CW01642222

#1
Bestselling
Author

Humanizing Leadership

Be the leader others
want to follow

LOUISE H. REID

Humanizing Leadership

ISBN-13: 978-1-990476-10-5

Published by: Expert Author Press

https://www.expertauthorpress.com/

Canadian Address:

1908 – 1251 Cardero Street,

Vancouver, BC, Canada, V6G 2H9

Phone: (604) 941-3041

info@expertauthorpress.com

This book is dedicated to **Julia Wagg** who continues to inspire me to be a better human being and leader.

To **my boys**. May you always know joy.

To **my parents**. Thank you for teaching me the power of kindness.

To **my sister**. Thank you for your ever-present light.

To **my love** whose faith and belief in me never waivers.

This book is possible because of you.

Humanizing Leadership
Be the leader others want to follow

Contents

Acknowledgments IX

A Letter to the Reader XI

Introduction: Advancing Technology & Humanity XV

A New Context

The Responsibility of Leadership

The Pillars & Practices of Humanizing Leadership

The Humanizing Leadership Model

PILLAR 1: LEAD SELF......pg. 01

Chapter 1. Identify Values & Vision 03

Lead With Heart

Discover Your Values

Clarify Your Leadership Vision

Chapter 2. Amp Up Your EI (Emotional Intelligence) 13

Soft Skills or Power Skills?

Amp Up Your EI

Chapter 3. Practice Mindful Leadership 23

Stress & Leadership

The 1-2-3- Switch Destress Exercise

How to Practice Mindful Leadership

PILLAR 2: LEAD OTHERS......pg.43

Chapter 4. Discover the Drivers of Motivation 45

Humans Through the Ages

Human Motivation

Lead Your Fear to Feeling

Fear is Human

Choose to Thrive

5 Universal Drivers that Simplify Leadership

Chapter 5. Unleash the Power of Your People 63

Play Your Position

The Magic of Being in the Zone

Use Strengths to Transform

Be the Change

Chapter 6. Dispel Myths that Limit Leaders 79

The Myth of Always On

The Myth of Multitasking

The Myth of Vulnerability

Chapter 7. Challenge Assumptions 105

"The Idiot on the Highway"

Why We Make Assumptions

When Assumptions are Bad for Business

The Power of Curiosity

Chapter 8. Identify Blind Spots **113**

Know Your Biases

Acknowledge Failure

Build Your Courage

Chapter 9. Foster Equity & Belonging **135**

Some Definitions

We Must Do Better

Intersectionality

Privilege

The Bridge of Discomfort

Cultivate a Culture of Authenticity

PILLAR 3: LEAD THE WAY......pg.159

Chapter 10. Pursue Leadership Mastery **161**

Ruther Bader Ginsburg

Jacinda Arden

Dr. Martin Luther King Jr.

Julia Wagg

About the Author **173**

Acknowledgments

I acknowledge that I am writing this book from my home built on the traditional unceded Algonquin Anishinaabe territory. The peoples of the Anishinaabe Algonquin Nation have nourished this land for millennia, and for that, I am grateful. Many walks through her woods have grounded and inspired me through this writing journey.

I also acknowledge that this book's concepts, materials and perspectives reflect my thinking, experiences, and reflections as a Caucasian, cis-gender woman of British heritage. I hold a deep concern for people, and although I have made deliberate efforts to foster inclusivity and embrace diverse perspectives, it is important to acknowledge that the western academic research (referenced in this book) and my upbringing and formal education rooted in North American culture inherently carry colonial biases. I will forever remain a student.

A Letter to the Reader

Dear Reader,

Thank you for being here! Before we dig into this important work on Humanizing Leadership, I'd like to share with you what inspired this book and where the deep yearning to birth it came from.

In 2017, I found myself in a period of intense introspection after the death of a friend, mentor, community builder, best-boss-ever, and amazing human being, Julia Wagg. In one word, she was brilliant. At the time I was working in a toxic work environment. Julia's passing caused me to deeply reflect on the role leaders play in employee well-being and success; on both human and performance outcomes. As I thought about the places I had worked and the leaders I had encountered, I noticed a common theme - widespread employee suffering at the hands of well-intentioned but ill-equipped leaders. This reflection and connecting of the dots took some time and turned out to be both a painful realization and a crossroads in my career. I am determined to be part of the solution and not contribute further to the problem. This realization coupled with Julia's premature and devastating passing clarified my commitment to the leadership work I do today and what inspired the writing of this book.

With over twenty years in Human Resources across multiple industries (telecommunications, aviation, non-profit, pharmaceuticals and utilities), I've personally reviewed the results of thousands of exit interviews. The top reasons people state for leaving include the need/desire for more training, the opportunity for career growth, and more performance feedback. The common denominator? The leader.

My mission and the purpose of this book is to end employee suffering by equipping and empowering you - the leader - to show up in a way that enables positive people and performance outcomes. Please don't be the reason an employee leaves a team or organization. By the end of the book, you'll have the information and tools you need to authentically show up, lead by example, and empower and inspire your teams. You will be equipped to see your employees for the people they are, uncover their meaning and purpose for being at work, and bring out the best in them through inspiration, not fear.

Generations coming into the workplace today expect to be able to bring their whole selves to work. It is more important than ever before for leaders to know what makes people want to produce, do a good job, and stay with a company. Understanding people is the basis for Humanizing Leadership and to understand others, you need to understand yourself first. You'll see in a moment, that's where we start - with you.

I'm inviting you to join me on this bold quest to humanize leadership. To make the transition from well-intentioned and ill-equipped to visionary and empowering. It's time for you to be brave, speak up and show people what you stand for. Are you ready?

Let's go!

TIP TO GET THE MOST OUT OF THIS BOOK

A top challenge in my 20+ years of HR is the low rate of training application from classroom to workplace, of the gap between "learn-new-thing and implement-new-thing". This book is designed to walk you through the process of awareness, learning, and application. There are questions throughout to stimulate self-reflection. I encourage you to answer them either in your head, in a Word doc, or in a journal. You can also access many of these exercises as a free download from my website: *www.humanizingleadership.com*. This book is aimed at awakening interest in the concept and how to's of humanizing leadership, so pause when you get to these points in the book where there's a question. Take a moment to reflect because this is where growth happens – in the work. Let it change you as you're reading. It's not a book to plow through, it's a book to grow through. Print the exercises, grab a notebook or your laptop, and capture your thoughts and answers along the way. Alternatively, if you're like me, you've got a highlighter and pen in hand and are writing directly in the book. Use the margins of the book, colour it up. A coach of mine years ago taught me a technique I still use today: take 3 different colour highlighters (I use yellow, blue and green). Yellow is for the passages that have me thinking "huh - that's interesting. I don't want to forget this"; blue for "I want to learn more about this later"; and green "I'm going to do/implement this." Using these highlighters helped me move through the the chapters with more flow and fewer interruptions with the confidence I had made note of the insights that mattered most to me. Finally, if you're a "I write inside my books" kind of person like me, please take a photo of a page and email it to me! It will bring me great joy to see my book being well-used and loved!

Introduction

Advancing Technology & Humanity

"I don't agree that there is a trade-off between doing good and profit. In my role, I not only create financial impact, grow the business, and create value - I create human impact. If the entire organization is focused on human impact, I know that we'll create the financial impact."

Mindy Grossman, President and CEO of WW International

Great leadership - the kind of leadership our world needs today - is not found in the head. It's felt in the heart. And while I define *Humanizing Leadership (HL)* as 'igniting the hearts and minds of others towards the achievement of a common goal', it's the heart part I see so very absent in leadership today. As such, it's where the focus of my book will be, and where I believe we have the greatest opportunity to restore the well-being of our people, bring more humanity into our workplaces, and create greater equity, inclusion, and belonging. And to do so in alignment with organizational vision, mission, and values. It's a tall ask and I know we can do it. We saw what was possible during the COVID-19 global pandemic. My faith was restored in leadership as I witnessed widespread empathy, compassion, and concern for others.

The 4 Cs of Humanizing Leadership

Compassion - The feeling and act of caring with someone in need; empathy in action

Character – One's defining mental and moral qualities

Courage – Inner strength in the face of fear or difficulty

Curiosity - The desire to learn, seek understanding and/or knowledge

Humanizing Leadership is the art and science of emboldening others created by the intersection of three disciplines: positive psychology, emotional intelligence (EI), and mindfulness with leadership. A blend of traditional with the new; of modern science and ancient wisdom. A convergence that sets us up to lead self with character, lead others with compassion, and lead the way with a set of tools and skills to integrate human wellbeing, engagement, and performance. HL builds the 4Cs required for effective leadership in our world today: compassion, character, courage, and curiosity. Simply stated, Humanizing Leadership is an approach that prioritizes both the advancement of humanity AND business outcomes. And what I know for sure is that when humanity is at the heart of our leadership decisions, it's a gateway to a better world.

A New Context

"Poor leadership could be the biggest barrier to a successful Fourth Industrial Revolution strategy."
(Deloitte)

The 4th Industrial Revolution (also known as Industry 4.0) is upon us. It brings change at an unprecedented rate and is fueled by new technologies, AI, genetic engineering, robotics, cognitive technologies, and the Internet of Things (I of T). Its impacts are far reaching in how we live, work, and relate to one another. Industry 4.0 is about the merging of these technologies with humans' physical lives, who we are, what we value, and who we become. These innovations are redefining what it means to be human and how we engage with one another. How do these innovations impact us as leaders and how we need to show up, at a time when tech is taking over? We're in very different times because of technology. Innovation quickly creates and forces change in jobs, skills, and people. As the world gets more digital, humans become more valuable. This means as we continue to innovate, developing human-friendly leaders matters.

When we combine technological advancements, shifting workforce demographics, social movements like #metoo and #blacklivesmatter, Corporate Social Responsibility (CSR) as a business imperative, a global climate crisis, COVID-19 pandemic, and the realization that diversity & inclusion is a moral and business responsibility, it's clear the old way of leading is not enough. The business world and social good worlds are coming together in a way we've never seen before. There's a movement towards not only shareholder value but businesses that are looking for shared value. INSEAD business school Professors Gianpiero Petriglieri and Jennifer Petriglieri, authors of "Can Business Schools Humanize Leadership?"[1] believe leadership has become overly depersonalized and sanitized and refer to this as a leadership industrial complex. "*Over one decade of corporate scandals, financial meltdowns and growing inequality has consolidated a disconnect with business and political leaders, as it is in the protests in the streets and squares around the globe.*"

This all means that the old industrial structures and styles of business and leadership need to evolve because they are no longer effective. We require a different leadership model, behavioral approach, and habits for Industry 4.0. Researchers at Deloitte agree "...as the transformation to Industry 4.0 continues, more business leaders are starting to see a bigger picture and a larger responsibility."[2] While the world is changing, the demands on leaders are changing. Our world is calling for a new type of leader. Are you ready to answer the call?

Drawing on leadership theories of Warren Bennis and Burt Nanus, in 1997 the US Army War College used the acronym VUCA (Volatile, Uncertain, Complex and Ambiguous) to describe the multilateral world resulting from the end of the Cold War. This term seemed to best describe four main factors they observed: the increasing pace of change, the difficulty in anticipating events, general instability, and unpredictability of the new reality. While the US Military used VUCA to describe or reflect on a specific event, in 2002 the business world caught on and because it described the business reality so well, it has since become common business speak. In the context of our boardrooms and VUCA it's no wonder there is increased stress and a sense of groundlessness as leaders are forced to make

---

[1] PETRIGLIERI, J. L., & PETRIGLIERI , G. (2015). Can Business Schools Humanize Leadership? *Academy of Management Learning & Education, Vol. 14*(No.4), 625–647. http://gpetriglieri.com/wp-content/uploads/2017/01/AMLE2015_Can_BSchools_Humanize_Leadership.pd

[2] Renjen, P. (2020, January 20). *Industry 4.0: At the intersection of readiness and responsibility Deloitte Global's annual survey on business's preparedness for a connected era.* Deloitte. https://www2.deloitte.com/us/en/insights/deloitte-review/issue-22/industry-4-0-technology-manufacturing-revolution.html?id=us:2el:3pr:4diGLOB1948:5awa:6di:012119:4ireadiness&pkid=1005744

decisions with no promise, and perhaps little confidence, about what the future holds. There is an increased complexity of the decisions we have to make and factors we need to consider (e.g. globalization, business ethics, and people factors like diversity and inclusion). And finally, speed. The pace with which leaders need to move requires quick decision-making otherwise they risk being outdone by a competitor or completely left behind in the marketplace. I have witnessed this perfect storm many times – leaders being called to make business and human decisions under pressure, a time crunch, with little information, and under stress. Leaders have not been taught to deal effectively with these competing demands and so what I have witnessed time and time again are decisions that leave a path of human destruction. This is what Humanizing Leadership will teach – the concepts and tactics to lead self in a way that effectively and responsibly leads others and leads the way.

The Responsibility of Leadership

Within this VUCA context, leaders have big shoes to fill! Bill George, a senior fellow at Harvard Business School, agrees and suggests that our VUCA world calls for leaders who have a different kind of VUCA: Vision, Understanding, Courage and Adaptability, all of which are embedded within the *Humanizing Leadership* Model and approach. While providing concepts and strategies to fill these shoes, I'd like to start with a term borrowed from medicine – nonmaleficence, which means "do no harm". Nonmaleficence is an ethical guidepost for those in our medical community and states that we should "act in ways that do not inflict evil or cause harm to others. In particular, we should not cause avoidable or intentional harm. This includes avoiding even the risk of harm."

This is a concept much needed in our leaders and workplaces today. While jobs may offer a level of financial security to its employees, avoidable and unintentional harm is being caused in other ways.

Consider this:

- 83% of US workers suffer from work-related stress.
- US businesses lose up to $300 billion yearly as a result of workplace stress.
- Stress causes around one million workers to miss work every day.
- Only 43% of US employees think their employers care about their work-life balance[3]

These are your people. They are in these statistics. And so are you, your friends, colleagues and family members. It's easy to look at numbers and want distance from them; but resist that urge. We cannot turn a blind eye to this anymore or wait for HR to launch a new program or corporate initiative. I am an ardent supporter of organization-wide initiatives that support human flourishing and wellbeing, and have led the development and implementation of many talent, inclusion, and wellbeing programs in my 20+ year career. I have learned that it takes a community of involved employees and leaders for these initiatives to take root and then bear fruit. The old adage "build it and they will come" is just not true in this case. Bottom line: yes to corporate wide policy and program development ***and*** to leadership support and active involvement. You – the leader – are the "boots on the street" for the corporate programs and initiatives. In fact, these programs don't work without you! As you champion these initiatives, you breathe life into them. You take them from a corporate initiative, policy and program that's written on paper to something that is alive, tangible and real. This enables your employees to know of them, access them, and benefit from them. That is the responsibility of leadership. It takes systems, processes and people to bring about change and this book is about you - the leader - and what you can do to revive and maintain the heartbeat of your team.

---

[3] Milenkovic, M. (2019, September 25). *42 Worrying Workplace Stress Statistics.* The American Institute of Stress. https://www.stress.org/42-worrying-workplace-stress-statistics

These people have entrusted you - their leader - to create a space where they can do their best work. Think about their excitement, engagement and energy on their first day. They are almost child-like in their curiosity and eagerness to learn and contribute. They show up each day willing and ready to learn and give what's required. And yet what I see is little by little, we chip away at the heart and soul of our people. It comes in many forms and it's so subtle. The power is in its consistency and frequency.

Let me share a few examples. It sounds like nit-picking, in the form of "feedback" over the format of a report, with no mention of the depth of research that went into its content. It could be not keeping your word, saying one thing to your direct reports, then turning around with a different message to your own leadership. Taking credit for the work of your team or not acknowledging their role. Or commonly cancelling a 1-on-1 meeting with your direct report...again. There's no malicious intent, yet the impact is significant. Think for a moment about when you started at your company. How did you feel on your first day and your first few weeks? Who was involved? What did they do? Time passes and then what happened? What changes? Can you see that it's not about the corporate program? It's far more personal than that. It really boils down to how your leader shows up, takes responsibility, builds the relationship, supports your on-the-job learning, creates clarity, communicates effectively, etc. This responsibility in fact is somewhat like that of a parent. I can vividly recall after the birth of my first child being discharged from the hospital. As new parents, my then husband and I were both excited and terrified at the same time! As we safely bundled our 8-pounder into his car seat and gathered our cards, gifts and flowers from the room, I looked at my husband and said "Are they just going to let us walk out of here with him? We don't know what to do!"

Despite this, we took responsibility to figure out parenthood, albeit scared as hell. We saw no other viable option.

Likewise, leaders often find themselves in situations where they don't know what to do including:

- Adapting to the pace of change.
- Balancing good leadership with meeting corporate deliverables.
- Developing and empowering employees.
- Building and maintaining trust with employees.
- Building a cohesive team.
- Navigating cultural differences.
- Supporting employee mental health.

When you take responsibility, have a willingness to learn and attempt new strategies, you too will figure out the best way to lead. Start by embracing your leadership role and taking action. As you show up with curiosity, you will find solutions and other times you may stumble upon the answers, like I did as a new mother. Like with parenthood, there are an abundance of resources available to support our learning journey - other leaders, courses, podcasts, and books like this one!

Leadership should not be taken lightly. Similar to parenting, it's a big commitment. I implore you not to choose this career path merely to get the salary raise, for perceived power or title. If you're currently in a leadership role, or readying yourself to step into one, be willing to take on the responsibility of creating psychological safety and job satisfaction for those on your team. Their personal wellbeing and career depend on it. This is the heart of leadership. Be ready to inspire them with clarity and competence and to show up with compassion, courage and character every day.

I dare say that if you're not part of the solution then you are part of the problem. As our world becomes increasingly VUCA, the need for humanized leadership increases. Our unpredictable life changes and workload realities often lead to stress, overwork, and overwhelm. The truth is, whether the stressors are directly linked to our workplace or not, we're seeing major leakage. Think of the last time you had a hard time getting the kids out the door to school or daycare – How were you when you showed up at work and raced to your first meeting of the day? Or when a parent or friend was seriously ill or passed away; how did it impact your presence at work? Some emotional leakage perhaps? We don't have a lot of downtime in our fast-paced reality and it's showing up in various ways, everywhere we go – our workplaces and homes alike. We all wear so many different hats, many with competing demands on our energy and time. What does this mean for you as a leader? That you're faced with needing to listen to and understand your employees' challenges and then to take it one step further by doing something about it. As a leader you have to do your job effectively so employees remain healthy, engaged, and productive. Yet our frantic pace at work and in life has become the new normal, which doesn't help us in the engagement and productivity department. Leaders today (and next gen leaders) have to navigate more challenges than ever. In these pages you will learn to effectively navigate our rapidly changing world and guide others through it with confidence and authenticity.

The Pillars and Practices (see Figure 1.0) within this book will serve you well if you have ***chosen*** leadership as your vocation. Whether it was an intentional decision or one that landed in your lap, you're mindfully choosing it now. Congratulations! A well lived life and great leadership is built through intentional action; they happen by choice not by chance. And with this choice comes great responsibility and privilege.

You see, people are not problems to solve. They are human beings to be heard, understood, supported, and developed. And leadership doesn't have to be as difficult as we make it out to be. We do love to overcomplicate things as human beings, don't we?

Throughout *Humanizing Leadership*, I'll share simple ways to connect with, listen to, and empower your employees. My goal is to provide you with a set of skills that can be used over and over again, in different situations and with all people including diverse backgrounds, interests, and styles. This approach will bring about a new way of being with one another; a way that opens the heart, expands what's possible, and creates greater space for common ground.

It Starts with You

What I know for sure is that it takes courage to step out of the mold and that we are at a point in our humanity that it's time to dig deep, do the work, and be the leader our businesses, communities and world needs. There is too much at stake now locally, nationally, internationally, climate-wise, politically, and socially not to. I believe there is greatness in all of us, but it takes curiosity to find it, character and compassion to nurture it, and courage to let it shine forth. You find the confidence to be great when you lean into your values and a purpose greater than yourself. Together they act as your North Star and help to motivate and propel you through the hard decisions and forks in the road where you will be tested. And so that is where *Humanizing Leadership* starts - with you. Let's shape the future – a better future - together starting now.

"It's not only OK to take your values to work; it's required," Henderson says. "A shared purpose can make firms both more productive and more innovative. But what's most important is that, in the end, [our values] are all we have.[4]*"* Henderson

The Pillars & Practices of Humanizing Leadership

Building sustainable and inclusive leadership necessitates emotional intelligence, mindfulness, and a deep understanding of what drives individuals to unleash their full potential and achieve excellence. It will all be covered in the pages of this book, organized into 3 Pillars and 10 Practices.

Pillar 1: Lead Self

1. Identify Values & Vision
2. Amp Up Your EI
3. Practice Mindful Leadership

Pillar 2: Lead Others

4. Discover the Drivers of Motivation
5. Unleash the Power of Your People
6. Dispel Myths that Limit Leaders
7. Challenge Assumptions
8. Identify Blind Spots
9. Foster Equity & Belonging

Pillar 3: Lead the Way

10. Pursue Leadership Mastery

---

[4] (n.d.). *THE TRIPLE BOTTOM LINE: WHAT IT IS & WHY IT'S IMPORTANT.* Harvard Business School Online. https://online.hbs.edu/blog/post/what-is-the-triple-bottom-line

The 3 Pillars organize the content into learning blocks, each building on the one before. The Practices within each provide you with the action steps to take. In doing so, you will not only revive the heartbeat in your current team; you will have the ability to navigate and effectively lead through the future seasons and cycles of business that we anticipate in Industry 4.0. Whether it's another unprecedented event like the COVID-19 pandemic and your workforce is suddenly scared, dispersed and working remotely, or your sector is impacted by political unrest, economic downturn, personal health problems and family challenges, the frameworks, tools and strategies within this book will support you in navigating all leadership scenarios with confidence, integrity, and impact.

Pillar 1: Lead Self

Lead Self is the first Pillar 1 of the *Humanizing Leadership* model. *Humanizing Leadership* is having the courage, compassion, character and curiosity to inspire and equip others towards the achievement of a common goal. Among aspiring and developing leaders, the aspect that often captures their attention is the final component of that definition: 'inspiring and equipping.' Many perceive leadership development as commencing at this stage. In fact, it couldn't be further from the truth. Drawing from my extensive experience spanning over 20 years in Human Resources, coaching, and leadership, I have come to understand that genuine, sustainable, and courageous leadership requires prioritizing inner work. Without this crucial foundation, the actions of leaders may seem hollow, insincere, and lacking authenticity. True leadership development begins with introspection and personal growth.

With that in mind, recognizing that every journey starts with a single step, we embark on the *Humanizing Leadership* journey, taking our initial stride – 'Lead Self'. You will be guided to pause, reflect and connect inward to examine your values, develop emotional intelligence, and lead more mindfully. We'll cover the first three practices here: 1. Identify Your Values and Vision, 2. Amp Up Your Emotional Intelligence, and 3. Practice

Mindful Leadership. The outcome? Greater self awareness, enabling you to build trust, collaborate authentically, and make better decisions. This will enrich all your relationships and experiences, at work and at play, whether remote or in person.

Pillar 2: Lead Others

While Pillar 1 (Lead Self) is about becoming ***self***-aware, Pillar 2 (Lead Others) is about becoming more ***others***-aware. With the tools and concepts from Pillar 1 in hand, we'll start applying them. This section of the book could be considered "on the job training". We will delve into the practical application of your acquired knowledge, encompassing emotional intelligence, values, vision, and mindfulness. This exploration will focus on understanding, effective communication with, and motivation of others.

This will significantly simplify leadership, making it more accessible and straightforward. With enhanced capabilities, you will possess the necessary tools to keenly observe the needs of others and effectively incorporate them into your relationships and decision-making processes. Through the Practices within Pillar 2 you will discover: the 5 Human Drivers and how to apply them in a way that simplifies and enhances your leadership; the myths and assumptions that limit leadership (and how to overcome them); and how to expand your perspective of and comfort with leading and nurturing diverse, inclusive teams.

Pillar 3: Lead the Way

The final section is about the expression of *Humanizing Leadership*; showing up, stepping up and speaking up as an inspiring, empowering leader. This is leadership mastery and is the culmination of your experiences, challenges, successes, and failures. It's not gained from achieving certain letters after your name, a title, status or salary. It's earned when you put what you've learned about self and others into impactful action. It's about unleashing your vision and getting others to ***want*** to come along for the ride. We'll walk through some well-known leaders who have exhibited these skills and made a deep, far-reaching impact in the lives of many. It's *Humanizing Leadership* in action.

I invite and encourage you to be curious as you read and lead. Adaptability and curiosity are traits that will serve next gen leaders well as we navigate this new world of work where remote and hybrid leadership skills are essential. Practice them as you go through the book so that in fact you grow as you go. You'll be amazed at the insights and possibilities that surface after asking simple questions; by inviting others into conversation. With genuine curiosity and open-mindedness, discussions can enrich both the relationship and the solution.

Leaders are not an island unto themselves, instead they are part of a larger system within a complex network of formal and informal frameworks, strategies, policies, and procedures. All impact how you show up and behave with your team. What I've learned and observed through my long career in the high-tech, aviation, non-profit, energy, and pharmaceutical sectors is that many leaders are searching to be better. They have a strong desire to lead their teams in a more humane and supportive way. I see leaders with a conscientious vision to deliver great results, while empowering and elevating the people on their teams. Humanized leaders want to show up in a way that is aligned with their values, while simultaneously achieving results. "How" to lead in this manner can be quite unclear, so allow this book and set of tools to be your guide.

Profit Story vs. People Impact

I have observed time and time again manager and director level leaders who experience stress and dissonance between the expectations they get from their senior leaders (the profit story) and the reality of how they need to behave and communicate with their teams in order to engage and support their employees (the people impact). Years in the high-tech industry have left me with many examples of how profit-story focused leaders ("I've got to make the quarterly targets/numbers"), with little or no mind of the impact on their people, leave a path of human destruction over time. Yes, short term results may be delivered, but employee wellbeing and engagement, longer-term productivity, and turnover all take a hit. This in turn impacts profit. An organization cannot have a healthy, long term profit story without caring about the people impact. The math simply does not add up. And yet, our people leaders are left to navigate this gap in between the profit story and people impact with little support or guidance from their own leadership or Human Resources. This space in between is where leaders are left to translate the language of business spoken in the profit story, and the language of people, spoken in the people impact. It's no wonder middle management is the most stressed out in our organizations.

This is where *Humanizing Leadership* concepts will build leadership competence so that people and profits are not seen as two opposing forces, rather they are recognized as two sides of the same coin. In fact, if leadership was a bird, I'd name one wing head and the other one heart. The bird cannot fly without both. Yes, business acumen and personal resolve are required to make financial, product and operational decisions – and I have met many leaders who excel in these areas. But in uncertain and changing times though, we need leaders to be more human too. With these factors of uncertainty and change now a constant in our world, accelerated since the COVID-19 pandemic, it is now a requirement that leaders care equally about the profit story and people impacts. To do otherwise is irresponsible, impossible, and unsustainable.

This book is for the leader with a conscience who values collaboration over competition. It's for the aspiring leader with the brains for business and the heart for people. You'll be equipped with the knowledge, skills and tools to lead in a way that develops people and generates organizational results. Everyone wins when we humanize our leadership and work culture because the right people join, stay, and deliver great work.

"Business's journey to balance profit and purpose is accelerating." (Deloitte Insights)

The world is calling for leaders who will do what is right, not what is easy. This often involves having to make unpopular decisions or to speak up against the status quo. While many of us would like to think that if we saw something, we'd say something research indicates most of us do not act, especially when in the company of others. In fact we maintain the status quo and then rationalize our inaction. I recall first learning about this concept, called the bystander effect, in first year university. I found it alarming. It struck me to the core. As a result, it is something I've never forgotten. In short the bystander effect is a psychosocial phenomenon that was catapulted into the limelight after the sensationalized 1964 murder of Kitty Genovese in New York City. At that time it was widely reported that as many as 38 people heard her cries for help during the attack but no one came to her aid. She was murdered shortly after. Unfortunately, the murder is true and thankfully the killer quickly found; however, the story about the many bystanders failing to act has since been disproved. What this tragedy did support is research on the bystander effect - what it is, why we fail to act in emergency situations when with others, as well as its implications to our world at work. In the work context, research has shown that being in the presence of others discourages an individual from intervening in an emergency situation, against a bully, or during an assault or other crime. Think about the last time you experienced a frustrating situation at work, a process inefficiency or common client problem. Who do you go to first? A trusted colleague? A leader? Employees typically speak to their colleagues (not managers or leaders) about work-related ideas, concerns, and opinions, often leaving leaders in the dark or with a false sense of what's going on.[5]

---

[5] Ekkirala, S., Hussain, I., Shu, R., & Tangirala , S. (2019). The Voice Bystander Effect: How Information Redundancy Inhibits Employee Voice. Academy of Management. https://doi.org/14 Jun 2019

You see, it's not in our nature to act out or speak out from the status quo; what is in our nature is to conform. Conformity keeps us within the "in group" which is safe. Safety – physical, emotional, mental – are what we are primed to prioritize above all else because our belongingness to a highly coordinated group is in part what has allowed our species to survive. This means when someone speaks up or acts out of alignment with the group, it rocks the proverbial boat and that unsettles the group. From an evolutionary perspective, those who speak up against the status quo hurt, not help, the group. Then these individuals become outcasts, no longer protected by the safety of the group. We see this still in the animal kingdom today, and humans are no different. If you come back to the present time, the same is true. We have policies that keep people in line. We want leaders to "tow the company line" even when they may disagree. Those who speak up against the "system" are exiled. This is critically important to know so that when you feel the aversion to speaking up or stepping out, you can notice it, accept it for what it is, and then take the right action (which is not always the easiest or most comfortable). Along with the other tools already discussed, the 4 Cs of leadership will help build your leadership confidence so that when you do bravely step up and speak up, it is deliberate, with integrity, and aligned with your values.

"Leadership is the act of acting on behalf of someone else or something bigger than yourself. Leadership is working with and supporting other people to use their gifts to accomplish a goal. Leadership is an act of love and caring—of making hard decisions and risking the blowback that comes from them."

Dr. Gretchen L. Schmelzer

Figure 1.0 – The Humanizing Leadership Model

This figure demonstrates how the 10 practices develop from the inside out, starting with Lead Self, Lead Others, and then Lead the Way.

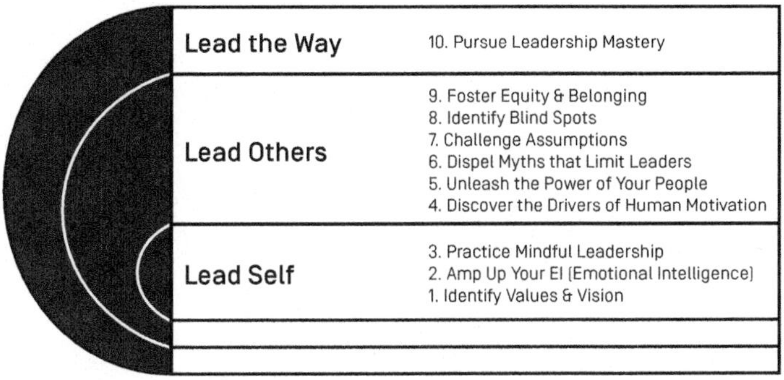

PILLAR 1: *Lead Self*

Chapter 1.
Identify Values & Vision

Chapter 2.
Amp Up Your EI (Emotional Intelligence)

Chapter 3.
Practice Mindful Leadership

To maximize your leadership effectiveness, critical thinking skills, and connection to others, you must understand your own ecosystem first. Whether or not you are a people leader at this stage of your career, we are all ultimately responsible for leading our own lives first. It is the prerequisite to effectively lead others and lead the way. This act of leading self requires you to connect inwards to your heart which is where you gain clarity of self and build character, compassion, curiosity, and courage - the foundation of Humanizing Leadership and what makes our intentions, words, and actions human vs transactional and procedural. While management is about controlling items or entities to achieve a goal, leadership is about inspiring, enabling, and empowering people to achieve organizational success. When you learn how to access and harness your spirit, wisdom, and knowledge, you are unstoppable.

CHAPTER ONE

Identify Values & Vision

> *Until they know their values and vision, people are rarely talking about what they're talking about.*

While technology has blessed us with its efficiencies and advancements, burdens have also been an unintentional result. There is pressure from consumers, industry, our organizations, and from our own leaders to do more with less and to do it faster. Competition has increased with globalization and offshoring, profit margins are tighter, and loyalty to the organization it seems, is a thing of the past. For employees, the experience is that business has become overly robotic, very sanitized and quite frantic. Work has lost its life force – its heart. I've seen it, felt it, and heard it. In our hyper-connected, "always on" online world, it seems ironic that we are less connected as human beings than ever before, even disconnected from ourselves. You only need to look at the staggering rates of depression and obesity in our westernized culture to witness how we're coping or not, as we seek to find answers and refuge in solutions outside of ourselves. It can come in the form of a pill, drink, quick fix or silver bullet. What if the answer is closer than you realize?

I've had great success with coaches in the past, experiencing the benefit of their help in getting from point A to point B in a significantly expedited manner, learning it is imperative to surround myself with people and professionals who've already walked the path. In February 2019 I hired a new business coach, award-winning author Joanna Garzilli. Early on in our conversations, I shared with Joanna where I was with my business and how I was working consulting contracts until my coaching business was more established. It was very much "I'm doing this until…" type-of-thinking. She asked:

"Why does it have to be either-or? Why can't it be yes, ***and***…"

I'm rarely at a loss for words but this time I was stumped. I had no reasonable or logical response. Instead I paused. I reflected for a few moments and what followed was a very enlightening conversation that explored the possibilities of *what if's*. Blinders fell away, my perspective expanded, and my business went through explosive growth. It was my narrow mindset that had limited me. While I'm still very focused on who I serve and why; taking a pause to examine my own thinking and beliefs has propelled me forward in a more personal and professionally rewarding direction.

With that I ask you to consider the "Yes, and…" approach in your leadership role. Yes, we must lead with our head; and also with heart. You see, the heart makes leadership human. It's what breathes life into our organizations and connects us with others.

Lead With Heart

Leading with heart means showing up for yourself and towards others with compassion, courage, curiosity and character. Notice that nowhere in this approach does it say to leave the head behind. We couldn't do that if we tried, nor would I want us to. I caution you against falling into a "black-or-white", "yes-or-no" polarized way of thinking. Almost all great life and leadership experiences happen in the grey – "the space in between" the extremes.

Speaking of extremes, in the mid-2000's I worked at one of Canada's largest and most successful technology companies, and sadly one that had a tragic demise - Nortel Networks. "...at its peak in 2000 (Nortel) accounted for more than one third of the total value of the S&P/TSX index, was the ninth most valuable corporation in the world and had employed more than 94,000 employees worldwide[6]…"

A team of researchers at the University of Ottawa spent 3 years studying what went wrong. I wonder…how could this tech giant who had top engineers, customer loyalty and market dominance experience so many setbacks that led to a painful death? And what could other leaders and organizations learn from this?

While researchers recognized and conveyed the complexity of the answer to "what went wrong", they did determine two catalytic decisions, both which showcased the weakness of leadership at the Board of Directors level. There are many interesting business and leadership learnings from Calof's report, but what's clear is they were all born from an arrogant mindset - one that appears to have lacked integrity in decision making, or decisions in alignment with their established values and vision: *"Canadian telecom giant Nortel collapsed because of losing the confidence of its clients amid a culture of arrogance and hubris."*

I respect the time, research approach and findings from this team at the University of Ottawa, but I'm also frustrated. How have we reached a point in business where we invest years and research funds just to recognize what we should already know - the imperative of truly comprehending and listening to our people?

We need to listen to the people doing the work; those who have been hired for their expertise and skills to bring a vision to life, and our leaders need to be equipped to hear, understand, and translate that into meaningful action. Here are a few of my key takeaways from this Nortel research:

1. **Listen** to your on-the-ground employees (engineers in the case of Nortel) and your customers. "…it was felt

---

[6] Calof, J. (2014). *An Overview of the Demise of Nortel Networks and Key Lessons Learned*. Telfer.Uottawa.ca. https://sites.telfer.uottawa.ca/nortelstudy/files/2014/02/nortel-summary-report-and-executive-summary.pdf

by many R&D staff that management rarely listened to the engineers and that, when they did, they did not appear to understand."

2. **Adapt and align** to the changing external environment and shift the culture as you go. Strategy and culture need to be aligned. "It was a complete departure from Nortel's established skills base, culture and history of developing its own products."
3. **Be humble.** Confidence is one thing, but there's no place for arrogance in successful businesses. "Nortel's sense of pride might have seemed to be a strength in the early days, but it created inflexibility in the latter days of the company. In fact, it escalated into hubris to the extent of making it especially difficult to absorb acquisitions, to quickly respond to market needs, and to accept and understand what customers wanted (largely as a result of the delusion of "we know better")".

I'll contrast that example with one from 2020 during the COVID-19 pandemic. Early in the pandemic, Jacinda Ardern, Prime Minister of New Zealand at the time, was being touted as possibly the best leader on the planet. *"She doesn't preach at them; she's standing with them,"* said Helen Clark, New Zealand's prime minister from 1999 to 2008. That statement alone is quite powerful considering the crisis she was leading her country through. Arden's style has been described as one with empathy at the core and she has the humility to listen to outside voices. What does this look like in terms of how she shows up?

While she hosted formal briefings, she also had frequent live Facebook chats to share information and connect informally with citizens. She was real and relatable; she showed up in a sweatshirt in one of her Facebook Lives after just having put her daughter to bed. She communicated often; sharing what she knew, while painting a realistic, honest and hopeful vision of the future. Along with her heart, she led with her head. That right there is *Humanizing Leadership* in action.

Discover Your Values

"Your visions will become clear only when you can look into your own heart. Who looks outside, dreams; who looks inside, awakes."

C.G. Jung

All too often we go about life on autopilot or default mode. It's the things we do without thinking. The literal meaning of autopilot is "a device that steers a ship, plane, or spacecraft by itself, without a person". Have you ever found yourself wondering:

- How did I get to work today?
- "Where are my glasses?" only to find them on your head.
- How many times have you said "Have a great day" or "I love you" and meant the words, but not really been present in the moment and actually felt the words as they left your mouth?

This is autopilot. And while it's highly effective at leaving brain energy for important activities and decisions, there's no present-moment awareness in it. There's no real intention or heart. It's simply following the path of least resistance, doing what's always been done, or even following the path others expect of you and doing so somewhat (or completely) mindlessly.

When I was 40 years old, I came face-to-face with years of living on autopilot and certainly from living more from my head than my heart. I had a great childhood; one that was full of achievement and happiness. Somewhere in the transition from adolescence to adulthood the achievement remained but the fulfillment was lost. With the busyness of earning a university degree, climbing the corporate ladder, getting the raises, and meeting the expectations of others, tunnel vision and autopilot left no room for joy, creativity or fulfillment. It was a slow, subtle and silent shift that it took years for me to realize.

On the outside, life at 40 years old looked pretty great, perhaps even Instagram worthy: married, fit and healthy, had 3 happy healthy boys, a great career, financial stability, and a nice house in a great neighbourhood. Then, as happens in life, a significant personal life event slammed me unknowingly into a brick wall called reality. The blinders fell away and I had no choice but to reflect. I recognized I had achieved all these "things", checked all the boxes that I had planned, and yet aside from being a mother, I felt pretty empty. I realized that while my heart had been giving me gentle nudges to pause along the way, my head rationalized them all, I stayed head strong, and I persisted. I plowed ahead according to the plan. When this personal tragedy happened. I wondered how I'd gotten so off course. How I'd moved so far away from my family, was in a job and professional field I really didn't, and was unhappy in my marriage. It marked the start of a new journey. An exploration of sorts. I paused and looked inwards after spending all of my life up until then looking outside of myself for the answers. I started with identifying my values, their importance to me, and how they showed up in my daily choices. I started here because I knew that my values reflected internally what I hold most dear.

From a workplace perspective, we see values written on business websites and on the walls of our meeting rooms. They may be included in job descriptions and interview question guides, embedded in the company's performance review processes, or part of an annual award program where recognition is given to employees who best represent and embody the values. *Whose values are these again?*

Right, the organization's.

We rarely give employees or leaders the time and tools to uncover their own values and see how they align with those of the company's. It sounds more like: "Welcome to our company! Our corporate values are x, y, z and here's how we expect you to live them. Your performance will be assessed against them and part of your annual salary increase will be based on how well you perform to these." When we work for a company, it's expected that we know and live by their values.

And yet so many of us don't know or live by our own.

Our fast-paced, achievement-oriented society where we seek external validation for our worthiness leaves little space to recognize the importance of looking inwards. Connecting to oneself can be scary – feelings live there. It's easier and emotionally safer to stay on busy street. This has led to an epidemic of disconnection where this one-sided conversation can lead to misalignment in what our leaders think, say and do. Consider if you walk-the-talk. Have you worked for someone who has? Who hasn't? And think about how each one impacted you, your engagement and performance.

While reflection like this can feel uncomfortable at times, have confidence in knowing that it's exactly where growth happens – in the discomfort. Expect it, lean into it, and learn through it. Your values become your own personal anchor.

Consider these questions as you reflect on your own values or visit www.HumanizingLeadership.com for a free download of the Vision & Values worksheet.

- What principles guide my decision-making?
- What matters most to me when faced with tough choices?
- When do I feel most aligned with my actions and beliefs?
- What do I want my legacy as a leader to be?
- What aspects of work inspire and motivate me?
- When do I feel the most fulfilled in my life - at work and personally?
- What behaviours and traits do I admire in others - at work and personally?
- How do I want to be remembered by my team?
- What fundamental beliefs shape my leadership approach?

Visionary Leadership

With your starting point clear – your values – where are you headed? Having clarity on where you're aiming will help you navigate to your desired destination - like putting in the coordinates of a GPS.

Vision shows us where we are headed.

Vision provides motivation and inspires us to keep on going.

Vision helps to keep us moving forward and move through obstacles.

Bring to mind a person whose influence on you has been profound. It may be a teacher, community leader, boss or sports coach. It's someone you would jump into the trenches with or follow to the ends of the earth because they asked. This is a person who, without their influence, you would not be the person you are today. Describe them. Consider what they said and did, what made them "great" in your eyes, and how they made you feel.

My person was Julia Wagg. What a bright, dynamic, inspiring mover and shaker she was. As my leader she let me fail, provided guidance when I struggled, connected me with people who could help me on projects, asked me how I was, knew about what was going on in my life, cared, wanted me to succeed, created space for me to be heard, opened up opportunities for me to practice and grow. We laughed, she kept me informed, she removed barriers, asked great questions, challenged me, delivered feedback that was hard to hear, and she helped me navigate the organizational context. Years later as I think about her, I can still sense how her leadership made me feel.

I conducted a small-sample social media survey to solicit some answers from my connections to *"Describe the best leader you've ever had"*. Here are some of the responses, revealing the powerful impact leadership can have on the lives of those leaders lead:

- "I think one of the most important traits I look for in Leadership is: Were they good followers at one time? Some of the other qualities are: Do they listen? Do they champion collaboration? Do they create a zero fault and blame environment? Are they Customer Success Focused? Do they Lead or do they Dictate? Are they EQ/IQ balanced?" S. Ahmed
- "A good leader is willing to work alongside their team. They're not too proud to talk about their failures or setbacks but share what they learned from it. Good leaders also hear suggestions from their team & others and give those people credit. A great leader celebrates EVERYTHING with their team members, no matter how big or small." K. Snell
- "Compassion. Faith. Love. Helping others. Gratitude. These are some of the qualities and practices that make up a former employer of mine. Best boss I've ever had and it's no coincidence that his business is flourishing." B. McCrae
- "Good leaders embody true empathy. A great capacity for listening and values their team while empowering them. Reliable leadership will always have your back and be willing to do what it takes to accomplish the mission of the work." F. Rodríguez
- "A great leader realizes leadership isn't about them, it's about their team. A great leader gets in the trenches with you, offers a helping hand and gives you space to make mistakes. A great leader encourages others to challenge them and great leaders thrive on not being the smartest person in the room!" L. Müller
- "To me, leadership is about shining the light on the destination. Those who arrive can then bathe in the light of ephemeral success." M. Patel
- "Someone who is authentic, genuine, sincere and trustworthy. Who can communicate both the good and the bad in a positive, uplifting way that moves people forward." R.Lee

- "Leaders should have purpose and a vision for the future. Their vision is crystal clear and the passion they have for it is contagious. Ambiguity in leadership is like a limp handshake. Clarity and passion is something I can get behind." A. Chung

How would you like to be described as a leader? What's your vision of yourself at your best? What do you do and say? How do you make people feel? Think about how you want to be remembered and allow that to help to generate a future vision of yourself to work towards. Great leadership happens by choice not by chance! If you would like help in identifying your values and setting the vision for your leadership, download the free Vision & Values worksheet from humanizingleadership.com.

"When we have a picture of a future we really want, we discover a path for change and the energy and enthusiasm necessary to sustain the process of reinventing ourselves." Richard Boyatzis, University Professor at Case Western Reserve University

CHAPTER TWO

Amp Up Your EI (Emotional Intelligence)

> *Emotional stupidity is one of the biggest causes of pain for yourself and others.*

In March 2020 I was at a *Women in Technology* event in celebration of *International Women's Day*. One of the participants at the table discussion I was facilitating expressed frustration over the lack of "people skills" her manager had. She described him as a micro-manager, disingenuous, and a poor communicator. Recently she had found out that a large project she'd spent months working on had been cancelled at a company-wide meeting - not from him. She was wondering how he could get promoted into a leadership position when he lacked what she thought were basic human interaction skills. This was not the first time something like this had happened with this manager, nor was it the first time in her career. In fact, all she had experienced in her 15 years in the field were leaders who were in their position because they wanted to earn a higher income, or because they were experts in their domain and were promoted. She was so frustrated and unhappy that she was even questioning her decision to be in the tech field.

Ugh! I can't tell you how many times I've heard variations of this story. It pains me to hear how people suffer at the hands of (usually) well intentioned but ill-equipped leaders. I can help ensure you're not that leader!

Power Skills

Let's agree on something - leadership is about leading *people*, in contrast to management which is about leading *projects*. This means that in order to lead others effectively - to create and share a compelling vision, inspire, and empower others - relational skills are the ticket. While this collection of skills has traditionally been labeled "soft" skills and include skills like communication, teamwork, adaptability, conflict management, they in fact are the price of entry for all leaders of the future. There's a negative connotation associated with the term "soft skills"; that those labeled as such are viewed as optional or of lesser value. I advocate a rebrand! In *Humanizing Leadership*, we call this set of skills power skills. Power skills are necessary relational skills - communication and interpersonal - required to successfully lead and thrive in our flatter, more interconnected, ambiguous and complex workplaces of today and the future. Many thought leaders, professors and experts in the field agree. Harvard Business Review article authors said "leaders with soft skills are the ones who will thrive in the next few decades of business[7]." Andreas Schleicher, widely regarded as one of the world's leading educational thinkers, said: "...in the fourth industrial revolution, arts may become more important than maths...We talk about 'soft skills' often as social and emotional skills, and hard skills as about science and maths, but it might be the opposite." He suggests that science and maths may become 'softer' in future when the need for them decreases due to technology, and the 'hard skills' will be "your curiosity, your leadership, your persistence and your resilience".

The Centre for Creative Leadership (CLC), a top-ranked global provider of executive education, has identified 4 fundamental leadership skills for the future (all power skills):

---

[7] Narayandas, D., & Moldoveanu, M. (n.d.). *The Future of Leadership Development*. Harvard Business Review. https://hbr.org/2019/03/the-future-of-leadership-development

self-awareness, communication, influence, and learning agility[8]. CLC indicated that a deficiency in any of these 4 skills will significantly hinder a leader's impact and success. Unfortunately, people are still being promoted into leadership positions based on hard skills (e.g. technical skills) and we continue to suffer. So as we hire and promote individuals into leadership roles, why aren't we preparing them more effectively?

Why EI

I encourage you to be the leader who ends this pain by focusing your energy where it will make a difference. Of course your hard skills are still important but let's now learn, master, and embody the skills that will make you invaluable.

"Since AI is expected to automate most of the task-oriented elements of leadership, particularly if they involve data-driven decisions, one would expect there will be an even bigger premium for leaders with strong people-skills and higher levels of EQ. That is because people will always crave human attention, empathy, and validation, which machines will not replicate anytime soon."[9]

In 1990, Peter Salovey and John D. Mayer coined the term *'Emotional Intelligence'* (EI) defining it as "a form of social intelligence that involves the ability to monitor one's own and others' feelings and emotions, to discriminate among them, and to use this information to guide one's thinking and action". These are power skills and highly likely ones you identified in your description of a positive influence/leader in your life. In the world of leadership, amping up your EI can be a gamechanger.

---

8 Leading Effectively Staff, N. (2022, November 24). *The Core Leadership Skills You Need in Every Role*. Center for Creative Leadership. https://www.ccl.org/articles/leading-effectively-articles/fundamental-4-core-leadership-skills-for-every-career-stage/

9 Chamorro-Premuzic, T. (n.d.). *As Long as We Associate Leadership with Masculinity, Women Will Be Overlooked.* Harvard Business Review. https://hbr.org/2019/03/as-long-as-we-associate-leadership-with-masculinity-women-will-be-overlooked

From the work and research done in the early 1990's, evidence-based emotional intelligence assessments were developed to measure emotional functioning in order to predict one's personal and professional effectiveness. The key difference between your emotional quotient (EQ) and intelligence quotient (IQ) is what they measure. EQ measures the ability to process ***emotions*** to come to sound decisions, whereas IQ is the ability to process ***information*** to come to sound decisions. Most of us understand and widely accept the concept of IQ, but not so much EQ despite research (and life experience) that suggests EQ is just as, if not more, important than IQ in determining leadership success. In short, EQ gives you a picture of how you react emotionally and socially. This knowledge helps you to recognize emotions in yourself and others, regulate your own emotions, and navigate emotions in all you do - in your relationships, communicating with others, and even in decision making. Considering leadership is about guiding others towards the achievement of a common goal, effective leadership can't exist without EI. Research shows this and in my over 20 years of experience in leadership and Human Resources I've witnessed it. It's that powerful!

Schools are starting to integrate social-emotional learning into their curricula but that's too late for those of us already in the workplace. Organizations need to keep pace and get on board with the evolving landscape. Just as a software designer cannot code without knowing the programming language a particular job requires; leaders can't lead to their best if they don't understand the language of emotions. The more we collectively understand the language of EI and how to apply it, the better our communications, relationships and leadership will be; creating a healthy and productive work environment with healthy and productive employees.

Determine Your EI

To reflect on your own emotional intelligence, take an assessment. There are free EI tools online that will ask you a series of questions relating to your emotional self-awareness, emotional management, social awareness, and relationship management.

a) Emotional self-awareness - How aware are you of your own emotions? Are you able to identify how you're feeling and name the emotion(s) and understand why you are feeling that way? Are you aware of the potential impact your emotions may have on others?

b) Emotional management - Managing our emotions helps us make good decisions - big and small - and maintain positive relationships. Are you able to effectively navigate and regulate your emotions when the stakes are high? Keep in mind that emotional management is about regulation, not repression.

c) Social awareness - How able are you to recognize and interpret the mainly non-verbal cues of others? Hearing spoken words is one thing, but tuning into and accurately reading the body language of another is critical. Non-verbal cues let you know how others are really feeling, how their emotions may be changing moment by moment (e.g. in response to something you say), and what's really important to them. When you communicate with others, do you pay attention to the unsaid, noticing emotional and social cues?

d) Relationship management - Do others leave interactions with you feeling seen, valued, and heard? Do you promptly address issues with others or do you tend to avoid them if there's a risk of conflict? When you communicate with others on tough issues (e.g. feedback or conflict) are you clear, direct, and kind? Do you engage in a way that helps (not hurts) relationships? When you navigate and nurture healthy relationships, others feel safe, understood, supported, and inspired to do their best work.

As you read the questions above, how'd you do? Just roughly. Consider gauging where you're at on a scale of low-medium-or-high on each of the 4 EI domains. For example, do you think you're low-medium-or-high on Emotional Self Awareness? What about Emotional Management? Social Awareness? Relationship Management? With this awareness and insight, you're able to acknowledge areas you're already strong in and identify opportunities for development. Keep in mind that emotional intelligence skills can be strengthened, so don't be hard on yourself if you're lower than you'd like to be. With this new information you can make informed choices about your development. Information and awareness is power!

Workplace Strategies for Mental Health, compliments of Canada Life, offers a free evidence-based online assessment that you can take. At time of publishing, the assessment can be found at www.workplacestrategiesformentalhealth.com[10] Considering the criticality of emotional intelligence in leadership today, I invite you to set aside the 10 minutes it takes to complete the assessment. Perhaps even now! You'll get a summary of your results along with specific actions you can take today to develop your EI. Awareness is one thing (I dare say it's the easy part) but knowing what to DO, and then DOING it, is where development actually happens. That's where our opportunity lies - in the doing.

When you discover the details of your EI and you commit to action, you amp up your leadership skills, abilities, and impact. You'll be able to recognize, navigate, and express the range of emotions you feel. You'll be able to notice and effectively respond to the range of emotions of others -positive, negative and everything in between. Emotional intelligence doesn't involve bottling up negative feelings, ignoring or avoiding the negative emotions of others, or faking nice when you're frustrated. Instead, it helps you to effectively interpret your own and others' emotions, and to appropriately express/respond to them so that everyone is

---

10 (n.d.). *Emotional Intelligence Self Assessment.* Workplace Strategies for Mental Health. https://www.workplacestrategiesformentalhealth.com/resources/emotional-intelligence-self-assessment

respected. This is at the heart of effective communications and leads to strong, positive relationships, sound decision making, and productive, healthy work cultures. For example, you're in a team meeting and one of your team members is multi-tasking, say on their phone or laptop, instead of participating in the discussion. You've noticed this before and in fact it's now worse since the onset of hybrid/remote work. You're feeling frustrated because you can tell they are not focused but you don't know how to react or respond. Do you ignore it? Do you bring it up in the meeting real-time? Do you raise it at your next 1-on-1? Emotional intelligence will help you to navigate these situations with greater ease and in a way that contributes to better outcomes. You'll be able to notice your own immediate reaction before responding, enabling you to mindfully choose how best to respond to the person and situation at hand. You'll be able to communicate more effectively, empathize, make aligned decisions, and navigate the complexity of stressful and conflict ridden situations. So like in the situation above - the multi-tasking during a meeting situation - with greater emotional awareness, you'll be better equipped to recognize your frustration, understand the cause, and regulate how you communicate so your response is helpful (not harmful).

Develop your EI

Combine strong EI with your professional domain expertise and I assure you that you and others will notice a difference in your leadership. It may not be right away, development does take time, but it will happen. And you will shine. You will be the leader that people refer to years from now when former employees are asked about the person/leader who most positively influenced them. If you want to be that legacy leader, one with integrity and authenticity who positively impacts people and profits, developing and nurturing your EI is critical. The alternative I have witnessed is the over-rotation and focus on creating short term quarterly results that leave a path of human destruction in their wake. You have come to the table with a level of cognitive intelligence. EI is the development opportunity for leaders. If you're looking for some ideas on where to start, here are a few:

- **Complete an EI assessment** either through the free resource on the Workplace Strategies for Mental Health website or contact someone who is EQi 2.0 certified and they can walk you through a robust psychometric assessment and support you in building a development plan. I'm a certified practitioner and you can find many others who are too! The benefit of an assessment first is that you can be more deliberate and targeted in the areas you choose to focus your development on.
- **Start observing how you feel** at various points throughout the day. Tying it to something you already do habitually makes it easy to remember. For example, when brushing your teeth, check in with yourself. Consider how you're feeling at that moment - physically, mentally, emotionally. It becomes easier the more you do it.
- **Practice observing your behaviour**, noticing how you react and respond in different situations throughout the day. In the busyness of our lives today, we often fail to reflect on how emotions rise up and cause us to automatically respond with little to no thought. Paying attention in this way can help us spot trends, some of which may be helpful and others not so much.
- **Be curious!** Oftentimes, questions are more powerful than answers. Questions provide opportunities for connection and can expand and challenge our thinking.
- **Recognize and celebrate the good.** Not toxic positivity, but instead genuinely noticing and acknowledging the good work being done, positive progress being made with a client, your kid remembering to unload the dishwasher without being asked. When you start paying attention to the good things that happen in your day you'll start noticing more good in your day. Your brain actually starts looking for it because you have changed

what you focus on. Gratitude and noticing "the good things" has been studied widely in recent years. It helps to build relationships and supports us in navigating adversity.

» **Acknowledge and explore the not-so-good.** Not all situations are good. Some are downright awful. Recognize your emotions without judgment. Reflecting on how you navigate these emotions and situations will help you in the future if faced with similar feelings.

If this sounds all a little overwhelming, remember that emotions are a rich part of what makes us human. The effort required to understand and cultivate emotional intelligence is so worthwhile. Because ultimately emotions are information. They cue us into our own needs and into the needs of others. As organizations embrace our evolving work landscape, leaders who exhibit emotional intelligence will flourish, bringing forth the rewards of these abilities. They will enhance communication and bolster trust by aiding their teams in managing emotions constructively. Collectively, leaders and their teams will be more prepared to overcome current and future challenges.

CHAPTER THREE

Practice Mindful Leadership

> *You can't eliminate stress but you can thrive despite it.*

We have established that emotions in leadership are not soft and optional, rather powerful and essential. The ability to be with "what is" especially in the face of challenging emotions is a powerskill; one that is honed through the awareness of emotional intelligence and the practice of mindfulness.

Spending time reflecting on and building inner awareness grounds you strongly within your personal leadership essence and values. It enables you to stand up with confidence and integrity when others shy away with fear and fragility, to show up with curiosity and compassion when others are closed-minded and unfeeling, and to speak up with courage and character when others do so with doubt and insincerity.

Heart is where these naturally occurring positive human traits that are necessary for leadership are born and nurtured. From here, all other leadership concepts can be learned and developed. However, there's another naturally occurring common human reaction that blocks many great people from fully realizing their leadership potential; something that is increasingly present in our fast-paced, 24-7 lives. In fact, it is getting worse.

Its name is stress. The good news is that when you have mastered the concepts within this chapter, you will have all you need to successfully lead and thrive regardless of the obstacles and stress that come your way, both at work and at play.

How do you learn to embody heart in the face of stress? The practice of mindfulness is an antidote to stress, but it does take a willingness to do something different.

Recognizing Stress

People have stress. And a lot of it. There is a continuous, daily barrage of personal and professional demands coming at us requiring our time and attention. It negatively affects our leadership, performance, communication, and relationships. We don't think well during stress, we automatically respond. We aren't as empathetic towards others, but more self-focused. It's how we are wired to respond in times of stress.

It extends beyond the office, into our home life and health too. In 2020, we added to that stressful baseline a global pandemic (COVID-19), political unrest in the US, George Floyd's murder (#BlackLivesMatter), job loss, and general global uncertainty and fear.

Developing your EI and learning the art of mindfulness will enable you to use and manage your own emotions in positive ways to better navigate and relieve stress. Listen to stress and it will show you what the whole you needs.

Robin, an executive director at a non-profit, started working with me because they had taken on a new project and needed help developing their strategic thinking skills (or so they thought). During our initial conversation they told me they were being held back by their poor ability to think on their feet in high stakes meetings, that when put on the spot to answer questions they weren't prepared for, they would get highly stressed and anxious. This was a problem because they presented regularly to the board. While they were very effective at presenting material that was prepared in advance, it went downhill when they felt put on the spot by being asked questions they hadn't expected. In these moments their mind went blank, they stumbled over their words, and they appeared unprepared. This had been going on for some time, and it was getting worse. They took the EQi assessment and also solicited 360 feedback. It told them a very different story from the one they were telling themself! The report and feedback provided indicated strong strategic planning and thinking skills. What also became clear was that their strategic/thinking on their feet skills were being masked in situations with emotion and stress. They realized that when overwhelmed and anxious, self doubt and worry crept in. With this new found self-awareness, coupled with motivation to address this challenge, we created a plan, they did the work, and they integrated a regular mindfulness practice. This meant when stress started to rise, they noticed it right away, and could take action quickly. With a few mindfulness tools at the ready, they were able to maintain focus, calm, and confidence in those moments where in the past they would shut down. This is the power of mindfulness and emotional intelligence.

In a leadership role, it is possible you are at an elevated level of stress much of the time, with asks and expectations coming at you from all directions. It is necessary to recognize when stress is present before we can guide others and consistently make good decisions. Then we can get out of our stressed brain response and into our thinking brain. "...threat, uncertainty, and anxiety lead us to make short-sighted decisions."[11]

If you have unhealthy boundaries or a high stress threshold, the signs of elevated stress may feel like an annoyance rather than a danger. Not only can this impede performance on tasks that require attention, memory, and decision making; an occasional headache can result in recurring debilitating migraines or a serious health challenge that takes you out of commission for months (or worse). There are serious health, relationship, and work-related repercussions when stress is ignored or left unaddressed. I urge

[11] Markman, A. (2020, March 15). Slow Down to Make Better Decisions in a Crisis. *Harvard Business Review.* https://hbr.org/2020/03/slow-down-to-make-better-decisions-in-a-crisis

you to watch closely for the perilous signs of stress, before it is too late. If you don't care for yourself, how can you take care of and lead others?

Stress: Friend of Foe?

I can hear some of you saying that stress helps you be at your best, that without it you can't get that presentation done or the edge you need to present well. And it's true that not all stress is bad! In fact, there's a name for healthy stress - eustress. Eustress is a form of stress that has a positive effect on health and psychological wellbeing. For example, receiving news of a job promotion that's aligned with your values, career goals, and strengths is exciting. Despite the pressure of more responsibility with longer hours, eustress can provide the motivation and mindset for improved performance in that specific role. The short-term anxiety and stress you experience before giving a big and important presentation can help you perform at your best. Running onto the road to rescue your toddler who has darted out of arm's reach is a positive, modern-day example of our fight-or-flight response put to good use.

The issue we have here in our workplaces today is ***chronic*** stress. It's this repeated and frequent exposure to stress that is wreaking havoc to our minds, bodies, work, relationships, and lives. Many scientists believe we were not built to endure the levels of stress hormones so many of us are subjected to.

According to Dr. Anil K. Sood .M.D. *"chronic stress can help cancer grow and spread in a number of ways…chronic stress increases the production of certain growth factors that increase your blood supply. This can speed the development of cancerous tumors"*.

Making the situation worse, the hippocampus; the part of the brain responsible for memory and emotion, can be damaged by stress! Stress actually damages the brain. According to the US Centre for Disease Control, up to 90% of visits to the doctor are due to stress and "In a large-scale study of over 3,000 employees conducted by Anna Nyberg at the Karolinska Institute, results showed a strong link between leadership behavior and heart disease in employees. Stress-producing bosses are literally bad for the heart."

Chronic stress is on the rise and something I witness day in and day out within the lives of employees and in our workplaces of today - a constant stream of inputs all requiring our attention, often-times coming at us at a rate faster than we are able to action. Many of us have heaps of responsibility but lack autonomy and authority, have fuzzy goals, and far too many priorities. Welcome stress! And doesn't everything seem to be a priority? Juggling priorities is an art unto itself.

What concerns me, as it should all leaders, is that we have become resigned to, and are far too accepting of, chronic stress. We've normalized chronic workplace stress and figure it's the individual employees' job to manage that stress properly. Chronic workplace stress is now synonymous with having a job. Additionally, we overlook, minimize or are unaware of its negative effects, thinking we should just "get over it" or do more self care. In actual fact, it is toxic, can lead to breakdown, burnout, and mental disease that, unchecked, can become a physical killer. We are in a stress crisis with our workplaces and many leaders within them, often unknowingly, are a significant cause.

Considering we spend the majority of our time of our working years at work (remote or in person), and because work is often cited as the #1 stressor for individuals, organizations and leaders have a responsibility to do something about this. Both our people and bottom lines are suffering the results of stress and it's well past time we take a more proactive approach to addressing this concern. During the global COVID-19 pandemic, if it wasn't already, mental health became a topic that could no longer be swept under the rug. No longer could we hide or ignore it in ways we could before. No longer could the crack in the foundation be quickly patched. The lack of care, time and attention on mental health – that "crack" in the foundation of our human spirit – became a canyon. And we had to wake up and take action. While the solution is complex and multi-faceted, requiring broad interventions at the national, political, legal, social, and organizational level, the power of good leadership as an intervention should not be underestimated.

Fight-Flight-Freeze ("The Stressed Out" Brain)	**Fight-Flight-Freeze ("The Stressed Out" Brain)**
In this state: • Automatic/default reactions rule • We tend to be impulsive & reactionary • It can feel emotionally distressing • Blood pressure & heart rate increases • Attention & perception becomes hyper focused • Word finding can be challenging • Quality sleep may elude us • Me-me-me is the focus (blinders are on) • Blood rushes away from the brain and to the muscles (making it hard to think clearly) • Hormones surge through the body causing feelings of anxiety • We worry "Am I safe?"	In this state: • We can be deliberate & intentional with our actions & responses • Innovation & creativity are unleashed • Collaboration with others is possible (from "me to we" thinking) • Access to better problem solving & decision making • Greater self control, reasoning & focus • Ability to access empathy & compassion • Ability to regulate your emotions • Can think about the future and think strategically.

Despite all of this, we expect ourselves and our employees to perform well under pressure with chronic stress.

Making Stress Your Friend

What if I told you that making stress your friend is as simple as 1-2-3? One thing I have learned in my life thus far, parenting 4 children, marriage, divorce, corporate layoffs and bankruptcies, great health, near death experiences, and everything in between is that the only certainty we have is what is in front of us right now. I've felt how scary uncertainty is; its unsettling groundlessness. And we know full well that in the future we will be faced with even more of it because just like the seasons change, as time passes, all things change. If we are struggling and suffering with the pace, uncertainty, and stress today, what will the future look like if we don't act now? What will the impact on our health, relationships and work performance be? I want to see more thriving in our world and with "1-2-3 Switch", you can start now.

Through all of my life's highs and lows, one of the greatest learnings for me, something so simple and always with me, is the power of my breath. Our breath is our ally and most of us have no idea of its powerful benefits. It's one thing that's always in our control. In a moment it can take us from stress and overwhelm, to calm and focus, putting us more in charge of our own physiology and into a place where we can make better decisions. The reality is that stress and calm can't coexist in our bodies. And your breath is the switch that turns off the sympathetic nervous system, aka the body's "fight-flight-freeze" response, and turns on the parasympathetic nervous system, the system of our body responsible for the relaxation response. Your breath is the gateway to undo the impact of a stressful event, restoring your heart rate and breath to normal levels and directing blood back to the part of the brain (prefrontal cortex) that is responsible for problem solving, creativity, impulse control, perseverance, and empathy.

"Mindfulness should no longer be considered a nice to have for executives. It's a must have."[12]

---

[12] Lazar, S. W., Congleton, C., & Hölzel, B. K. (2015, January 8). Mindfulness Can Literally Change Your Brain. *Harvard Business Review.* https://hbr.org/2015/01/mindfulness-can-literally-change-your-brain

During stress (sympathetic response) blood and energy is immediately sent to parts of the body and brain that will allow us to react and move quickly to help us escape from danger. And thank goodness for that! I recall many-a-time appreciating that immediate, automatic response. Like when my 3-year old son darted out in front of traffic and my reaction to scream scared the driver who quickly responded by slamming on the brakes. However, during stress when our sympathetic system activates, our parasympathetic does not. It's one or the other. When stress is on, calm is off. They do not co-exist. Why should you care? Isn't a little bit of stress good? Well, it can be, but we are living in a world of chronic stress and it causes ill health, lowers immunity, and decreases compassion, human connection, and work productivity.

The breath is like a light switch. Just as flipping on the light switch illuminates the room, allowing you to fully see what's in there, the breath switches on the part of the brain where intelligence and empathy are found allowing you to think and connect with others. It expands our perspective. Without the switch on/the breath, you cannot see.

Considering the part of our brain responsible for things like relating to others, compassion, courage, and critical thinking – all needed in our leaders today – is only accessible in our relaxed, calm state (i.e.parasympathetic) it's a problem for those leaders who live in stress mode. We need leaders to share and make decisions from calm, not chaos. And intentional breath using the *Humanizing Leadership* technique called "1-2-3 Switch" is the tool, allowing you to choose to be proactive (not reactive) in your approach.

The "1-2-3 Switch" Exercise

This is a very simple and effective tool to destress in any moment when you need it. You can do it anytime, anywhere and no one will even know. First read the simple steps below and then give it a try.

- Sit in a comfortable position with your back straight and shoulders rolled back and relaxed away from your ears.
- Pause and bring your attention to where you are right here and now
- Inhale for 3 slow counts
- Hold for 3 slow counts
- Exhale for 3 slow counts
- Hold for 3 counts
- REPEAT 3 or 4 times
- SWITCH – notice how you feel compared to when you started the exercise.

✎__**TIP:**

If imagery helps you, as it does me, imagine drawing a box with the breath, so as you inhale, imagine in your mind's eye a line being drawn straight up, as you hold your breath draw a horizontal line across, as you exhale draw vertical line down, and with the final breath hold draw a horizontal line to complete the square. This imagery along with your breath brings you to the present moment, helps your mind wander less and focus on the task at hand or person in front of you. This is commonly referred to as "box breathing".

IMPORTANT NOTE:

Your mind ***will*** wander. It's what our minds do! You are not trying to still your mind, you're trying to turn down the intensity, stress, and feeling of racing, anxiety or overwhelm. 1-2-3- Switch brings you back into a state where you notice all the thoughts in your mind and actively choose which ones to let go and which ones to pay attention to. With a regular mindfulness practice, you are training your brain to more effectively focus, think, collaborate, empathize and make strategic decisions. When your mind wanders, simply start again, bring your attention back to your breath and draw the imaginary square.

So what's happening here? Well quite a lot. But here's the basics and what you need to know. The breath is your switch from stress and overwhelm to calm and present focus. Your breath turns ON your "rest & digest" body system where thinking, problem solving, empathy, and collaborating with others happens while at the same time turning OFF the "fight-flight-freeze" system. It is a simple process of waking up your senses so you can lead with greater wisdom and in a way that feels right to you. It allows you to listen and respond to the needs of self and others and respond in a way that is healthy and empowering as opposed to automatic and habitual. Continued attention to noticing your mind wandering and then gently bringing your focus back to the task at hand is actually building the neuroplasticity of your brain; it literally changes your brain. And it makes you a nicer person who makes better decisions.

What this conscious breath can do is open you up to an entirely new approach to leadership. It can provide you the opportunity to experience others as human beings in a world and business reality that are wrought with so much fear, loneliness and separation. We can build bridges to overcome conflict and distance. We have relational networks in our brains, and these reside in the newest, most evolved part of our intelligence.

These networks enable us to feel empathy and a connection to one another. Greater present moment awareness, or mindfulness, allows you to tune into what's going on right now instead of focusing on what's going to happen next. It clears out the clutter and noise in your mind and enables you to see things clearly. It's where creativity, compassion, connection, and clarity is found. The data is in and the science is clear, which spoke to me in a way that the benefits never had before.

"1-2-3 Switch" brings you into the present, a way of purposely bringing your attention to experiences occurring in the moment without judgment. It allows you to be intentional about what you pay attention to, enabling you to be mindful of how you apply the facts, context, past experiences to judge and decide how to proceed and take action. It connects you with your values and vision so you can respond with your head and heart in a way that supports people and business.

The literal Chinese translation for the word mindfulness is "present heart". Engaging in this present moment focus, getting out of the stressed body and into the calm heart has significant, far-reaching benefits: improves focus and concentration, lowers stress, relieves pain, improves your immune system (stress wreaks havoc on all body systems), can help prevent depression relapse, improves sleep, improves relationship s and leadership. Research has validated that mindful practice improves a person's ability to collaborate, listen to others and communicate effectively, all essential skills in leadership.

You can download the 1-2-3 Switch exercise from humanizingleadership.com

The Benefits of Intentional Breath

Do not underestimate your breath's power as a way to stabilize you. There are a multitude of personal and leadership benefits to breathing consciously. The likes of Google, LinkedIn, Nike, Apple, Harvard embrace mindfulness and in fact offer training to their employees. Some of the benefits to the individual are:

- Helping you re-center, refocus and reclaim your focus, concentration and attention. From this state, you'll be able to successfully prioritize important work for your day and follow through on your current goals; you'll be able to recognize, regulate, and appropriately respond to the emotions that arise in you and others.
- Enjoying those around you. Your breath is that switch that transports out of the chaos of your busy brain and into the calm and clarity of your thinking brain. All in a few, intentional, deep breaths. You'll notice others for the value they bring both personally and professionally. This is the magic of human connection!

Studies have also shown strong evidence that being in the moment, without judgment, changes the brain in regions associated with self-regulation. This is mindfulness: the ability to temper responses, suppress knee jerk reactions, and understand and regulate the various emotions we may feel throughout the day.

1-2-3 Switch is a powerful tool that you always have at the ready to help bring you into the moment, to balance your emotions, manage stress, and make better decisions. It creates mental toughness and resilience. You can have all the skill and intelligence in the world, but without mental resilience, in times of stress, change, and ambiguity you'll have little ability to access it. I challenge you to try "1-2-3 Switch". What do you have to lose other than a little bit of stress?

Mindfulness and meditation have become mainstream over the last number of years, and for that I'm really thankful. I first heard those two terms in 1997 when I studied Wellness at college and I'll admit, I was very wary. My science mind and my nuclear physicist dad were skeptical, so much so that it wasn't until I turned 40 that I dusted off the idea of mindfulness and meditation and really gave it a go.

Why at 40? You may recall from my story earlier that at age 40, I was in a state of burnout, unhappiness and depression. I had let it go too long. I had to do something which involved a combined approach of medication and meditation, along with exercise, fresh air, friendships, and major mindset work to ditch busy, guilt, fear and shame. Better late than never, so the saying goes. It was through this unraveling and rebuilding; a breaking down of sorts that enabled a breakthrough - that I reconnected with my inner ability to self-regulate, and notice stress before it accumulated to such a load that it would take me. And what I learned was a set of evidence-based tools and skills that not only improved my wellbeing, but my performance and leadership too.

While I'd like to think that each of you are going to put down this book and become regular meditators from here on out, I don't expect that to be the case. Instead what I'd encourage is for you to be curious while I share with you how I have come to use meditation and mindfulness as a tool every day in my life beyond my meditation pillow. And perhaps, just perhaps, you'll give it the old college try.

"Practicing mindfulness for 10 minutes a day can enhance leadership effectiveness by helping you regulate your emotions and make sense of previous experiences"[13].

---

[13] Pillay, S. (2017, May 12). Your Brain Can Only Take So Much Focus. *Harvard Business Review.* https://hbr.org/2017/05/your-brain-can-only-take-so-much-focus

Look, Listen & Feel

This is what you do in the space between noticing an emotion and responding. Mindfulness takes you into that space where you can process more thoughtfully and intentionally what to do or say. It provides the opportunity for you to show up authentically and aligned with your vision and values.

Going back to my teen years as a lifeguard, in our monthly training sessions we would practice a variety of life-saving skills and situations to ensure we were prepared and ready to act when faced with a real life emergency at the pool. In a rescue situation where we came upon an unconscious victim, we were taught to use the "look, listen, and feel" approach. We would ***look*** around us to assess the situation to see if we could identify what had happened while also looking at the victim to see what they may need in the form of first aid or CPR. We would ***listen*** to the victim and if unconscious we'd look to see if they were breathing (is their chest rising and falling) and we would ***feel*** for other vital signs (pulse). We'd make use of our senses before taking action.

We can use this same, simple approach in our leadership. Bring to mind a time where you walked into an unexpected stressful situation at work. Perhaps one comes to mind quickly. It may come in the form of an overnight email where everyone under the sun was cc'd and it was the one night you decided to give yourself a tech break. You're frantically scrolling through all the chain of responses and notice your VP has chimed in a couple of times. Your heart rate accelerates, palms are sweaty, mind is racing.

With that situation top of mind, here's how to quickly move from chaos to calm in order to best make decisions and guide others. This process is repeatable and useful in any work or personal situation you may encounter.

1. 1-2-3- *Switch*. Breathe in and out a few full, deep breaths to slow your mind; and find a state of calm with intentional

thinking. From a mindset of awareness, you can say goodbye to panic, tunnel vision thinking, and automatic reactions.

2. *Look & listen*. This is an introspective step, which means you're not yet responding; you're not making a frantic phone call or sending a "reply all" email. Instead, you're using your senses to gain more information and facts about the situation in front of you. The key action words are ***observe*** and ***inquire***. These questions will help you identify the scope and severity of the problem before deciding possible actions to achieve a solution.

- What's happening right now?
- Is there a metaphorical "bleeding neck" that has to be addressed immediately? If so, ACT NOW!
- Can I take some time to get more facts?
- Who's involved?
- What do I notice?
- Is it really a 911 or is it a bunch of people working hard on a difficult problem who are in the fight or flight response?
- What else?

Despite the high intensity or flurry of activity you will notice that most of the time, it is not an emergency scenario. By asking yourself "What else?", you are taking charge of your mind in a powerful way. You're allowing yourself time and space to be curious which helps avoid reacting in the moment to what was in front of you. It steers you away from unnecessary stress and equips you to do exactly what's needed with minimal disruption.

You're still in the information gathering phase but this is more active, asking questions of others to gain a fuller understanding of the situation. The key action in this step is curiosity. Keep in mind that to date, you have only your perspective or version of the story. In a state of calm, with your prefrontal cortex activated, you're able to widen your perspective and consider options, feedback, and perspectives of others in a collaborative way. This open-mindedness is critical, which is why "1-2-3 Switch" is always the first step, enabling you to think fully and deliberately and not automatically react. Depending on the scope and severity of the situation, this step may take minutes, or it may take months. Make sure your scope of inquiry matches the severity of the problem!

- Ask questions.
- Listen for answers.
- What have they tried? What else?
- What has worked? What else?
- What hasn't worked? What else?
- What specifically do they need your help/advice/expertise on?

Remember you're the leader to make decisions and guide others towards a greater goal. You're not a firefighter anymore. Resist the urge to pick up the firehose.

3. *Feel.* Emotions are information and in fact the biggest part of what makes us human. While for some the idea of "feeling" in the workplace can cause an allergic reaction, it is part of the human experience. Consider for a moment what a day would be like without joy, anger, fear, anticipation, uncertainty. Emotions point us in the direction of either something to avoid because it's dangerous, wrong, or harmful to self or others OR towards something that will have a reward. They motivate us to act in a way that allows us to survive and thrive, spurring us to take action that ensures our survival and success. From a Humanizing Leadership standpoint, emotions help us to connect, share, bond, and trust. When emotions are identified, regulated and communicated intentionally,

we can elevate our impact as a leader. It is absolutely the difference maker in leadership, so let empathy and curiosity be your guide here as you assess the emotional waters of every situation.

- Based on what has been said or done, what is the emotional temperature of the situation?
- Based on what's NOT been said or done, what does it suggest about the emotional temperatures of the situation?
- How does the emotional temperature of the situation impact how I need to respond?

We live in a very action-biased society and I observe very smart, well-educated leaders jumping into solving problems without fully assessing the situation. Imagine a lifeguard coming upon a person lying on the beach appearing unconscious, not assessing the environment or situation, no calling out to see if they need help, no "look, listen, feel" to identify if they are breathing or not, instead immediately beginning CPR; blowing into their mouth and doing chest compressions only to find out the person was taking a nap. And yet we do this in business. Every. Single. Day.

Moving to action without being mindful leads to a multitude of problems such as:

- Projects failing or late due to lack of fulsome consultation stakeholders.
- Stakeholder groups missed from consultation altogether, or not consulted enough through the process such that the project delivered, no longer met the needs of the client.
- Not listening to those on the ground doing the work or using the services; a "we know better" attitude.

Earlier in my career I worked with a company whose IT department was launching a large scale, cross departmental project. They consulted well with all stakeholders upfront, but went away for months working their craft, only to emerge with a solution that while solving the problem from months ago, did not address the reality that business had since evolved and the solution no longer met the needs. While the "Look, listen, feel" approach may have been at the front end, they failed to reassess the "victim" and give the life-saving first aid that was needed as the situation changed to keep the person alive.

Great leaders are curious, open-minded learners. They listen for the purpose of understanding, gathering new information, connecting and empathizing with others, and to make better, more informed decisions. This is not easy or automatic for most of us as we move through the world subconsciously looking for and noticing information that confirms what we already believe to be true. However, like the curiosity of a child asking *why,* humanized leaders embody a beginner's mindset; a mentality that even when studying something at an advanced level, they approach leadership with the openness and curiosity of a beginner.

Respond with the Platinum Rule

When you begin to look, listen and feel, you will likely feel discomfort doing business because you are becoming aware of what is unspoken – the emotional content of the situation. However, you will start to improve your leadership communication skills as you lean into this discomfort and in doing so you discover the styles and preferences of others. We are all leaving clues whether we are aware of this or not and when we conscientiously look, listen and feel, we can clearly see and hear the clues others leave behind. These clues tell us what others need or want. However, in our increasingly busy world, spending more time in our overloaded brain than in our thinking brain, we tend to assume other people are like us. In fairness to us all, it's human nature to assume others see the world as we do. We see the world through our lens, which is informed by our experiences, preferences, background, upbringing, and so on. And we tend to believe this is THE world view as opposed to OUR world view. When we realize someone doesn't think like us or see the world as we do, we bump up against resistance, usually leaving us either unaware or uncertain as to how to respond. That's when friction or conflict can arise. Recognize the resistance and instead of getting defensive, become curious. Apply the "1-2-3 Switch Rule", then look, listen & feel.

Treat others the way ***they*** want to be treated. The idea of leaders responding to the unique needs of others has become pronounced during the COVID-19 pandemic, spotlighting how different our lives and needs really are. Meeting others where they are at is an approach in stark contrast to the common The Golden Rule of "treat others the way you want to be treated". I'm sure all, or at least most of you, have heard this phrase at one time or another. If I could run to the top of the highest mountain for all of the world to hear, I would bellow – ENOUGH WITH THE GOLDEN RULE!

Why would I want to be treated the same way as you? I've learned that treating people fairly does NOT mean treating them all the same. I'm referring to everyday interactions and communication, coaching approach, solutions offered, flexibility and creativity in meeting human needs, etc. For example, I love hugs. Physical touch is how I naturally like to connect with others in all parts of my life. It's an expression of my appreciation and fondness for them with a touch on the shoulder, an encouraging rub on the upper back, or a hug. Speaking of hugs, I actually love hugs in the workplace. There I said it. Gasp, I know! An HR person saying hugs are ok? Actually, not quite. Life's not black and white, as much as we may wish it was, and neither are the nuances of *Humanizing Leadership*. In fact, I'm suggesting that it's ***in the nuances*** of situations and relationships that we find joy, creativity and connection. Back to the hugs. Please know I'm referring to appropriate ones of course. Some of us know the difference, some of us don't. And if you're not sure, err on the side of caution and save the hugs for your personal life.

All this to say, even though I appreciate hugs, I wouldn't hug a non-hugger. I wouldn't force my hugs on someone else just because I like them. I wouldn't hug a new person on their first day on the job even though I would love to get hugs on my first day of work. Just don't do it! While this example may be somewhat laughable, I admit, we all unconsciously do variations of this. We tend to treat others the way ***we*** want to be treated.

Instead, flip it. Pay attention to the cues of others – their words and their non-verbals – and treat them that way. This is the Platinum Rule - treat others the way ***they*** want to be treated. In other words, meet them where they are at. It takes the guesswork out of the situation and it works every single time! There is no one-size- fits- all, but what I know for sure is that when you are mindful and tune into others, they leave clues through their words, their body language, and their tone. Become a student of your people - study them, learn and care about them, and then how to respond will become clear. This is an example of the "grey" in leadership. There are no black and white answers that can come to you from a policy or a spreadsheet. Those may be great tools, but they cannot replace the humanity inside each of us. Embody the *Humanizing Leadership* philosophy. Enjoy it! There's magic in our connection with others. And in this magic we have the power to increase our ability to influence others, motivate our teams to achieve great results, and develop talent - capabilities needed in ***all*** great leaders.

PILLAR 2: *Lead Others*

Chapter 4.
Discover the Drivers of Motivation

Chapter 5.
Unleash the Power of Your People

Chapter 6.
Dispel Myths that Limit Leaders

Chapter 7.
Challenge Assumptions

Chapter 8.
Identify Blind Spots

Chapter 9.
Foster Equity & Belonging

Leadership is a people business. That means that to do it well - to collaborate, influence and inspire - you need an understanding of what drives, encourages, and motivates people. In this section of the book you'll learn and see how to apply the "5 Drivers of Motivation" to understand how to motivate employees to do their best work. The outcome? Dramatically simplified leadership. While we are all unique, there are some common drivers that once understood, act as keys which unlock the door of employee potential and performance. To get there however, you'll need to learn about some natural human tendencies, how they show up at work, and strategies to apply this knowledge when connecting with and leading others. It will accelerate your leadership effectiveness and impact in this increasingly complex and diverse global business landscape, giving you a competitive edge in building and inspiring talent to execute and achieve.

CHAPTER FOUR

Discover the Drivers of Motivation

> *If you want to keep people motivated, find out what drives them.*

Humans Through the Ages

"You can take the person out of the Stone Age, evolutionary psychologists contend, but you can't take the Stone Age out of the person." Nigel Nicholson

Human beings have existed for millions of years; about 200,000 of those years as homo sapiens (that's us!). While our brains have physically grown in size, and our intellect along with that, modern humans remain very much emotional and instinctual beings. That older, primitive part of our brain still exists within us and is at play every day of our lives, in every decision we make and experience we have. ***Yes***, intellectual, ***and*** emotional. What we so cleverly do now is use our intellect and language to rationalize much of our emotional and instinctual landscape subconsciously. And this shows up in every part of our life, both personal and professional.

Human needs really haven't evolved all that much over 200,000 years - like our need for safety, love, belonging, purpose - but a lot in our physical environment has changed. We live in modern societies with laws that govern us, homes that keep us warm and safe, jobs that provide for us, grocery stores to feed us, and online shopping to clothe us. So while our physical world is vastly different from our hunter-gatherer ancestors, much within our brains - our innate drives, wants, and needs - remain unchanged. What does this have to do with leading others? Everything!

In my university psychology classes I was fascinated by Maslow's *Hierarchy of Needs,* McCelland 's *The Learned Needs Theory*, and Herzberg's *Two Factor Theory*, among others. My takeaways were simple. There are deep psychological and environmental needs all humans require to survive, develop, and be motivated, successful, and satisfied. There's no one single theory that's universal, but what is widely accepted is that together they provide insights into human nature, and how we can motivate and lead others. You can't lead effectively without knowing this, albeit some have an intuitive ability to "read" others so may not be able to articulate it. You might be familiar with leaders who possess the remarkable ability to understand and connect with others, effortlessly adjusting their approach while maintaining authenticity. If you don't currently identify with such leaders, there's no need to worry. It is widely acknowledged that leadership can be learned and developed by anyone.

Lacking this knowledge and skill is akin to driving towards a destination without a map. However, when you remain grounded (recollecting 1-2-3-Switch), attuned to your emotions, and lead others while incorporating these essential drivers, the journey becomes much clearer and less mysterious.

5 Drivers That Simplify Leadership

"Not everyone is like you" I said to a coaching client. There was a long pause followed by a moment of realization. Through our coaching sessions, my client gained a profound realization that she had been treating her employee based on how she personally desired to be treated. However, she had neglected to pause and contemplate what truly mattered to her employees or inquire about their needs and preferences.

As an executive in a national non-profit agency, my client held a personal value for increased levels of responsibility and recognition through promotions as a means of acknowledging and appreciating a job well done. After talking with her about the 5 Drivers - I am safe, I matter, I belong, I have meaningful work, I am growing, learning, and/or achieving - she decided to talk to her employees about what ***they*** valued. What mattered to them personally. What made them feel good about their work and accomplishments. How they liked to be appreciated. In this moment of clarity, my client realized that her employees' drivers were in fact different from hers. In both subtle and more overt manners, her employees had been communicating their priorities to her all along, expressing a strong appreciation for work-life balance, a focus on continuous learning and knowledge deepening (rather than mere career advancement), and the immense motivational power of words of appreciation. During that conversation, my client had an important realization about the significance of mindfulness in her interactions with employees. She understood the importance of being fully present, setting aside distractions such as preparing for upcoming board meetings. She recognized the value of genuinely listening to her employees' needs and preferences, being curious instead of assuming they shared her own desires and values. Moreover, she acknowledged the importance of responding to them in a manner that added value, free from defensiveness or deflection. The utilization of the 5 Drivers proved to be a valuable tool for my client, enabling her to establish meaningful connections and cultivate talent within her team. As a result, both individual and collective outcomes experienced notable improvements.

While the 5 Drivers draw support from research and conventional wisdom, it's important to note that they do not represent a strictly scientific model but rather a conceptual one. They provide a framework, language, and tool for you to effectively apply in your efforts to understand and connect with others. This requires intentionality, emotional intelligence, and being fully present in order to perceive others from their own perspective, rather than solely through your own lens. It takes what experience, research, and intuition has told us about human needs and motivation and presents a conceptual model for application by individual leaders. It makes the research more accessible thereby increasing your ability to understand and meet the emotional needs of others. This then fosters an environment that cultivates healthy communication and promotes effective teamwork, establishing a positive climate within the organization.

It is important to note that the first three drivers are foundational and essential for human survival, while the last two are more dependent on specific situations and contexts. The significance of the final two drivers is contingent upon the fulfillment of the first three needs and may or may not hold importance to an individual in their work context. This is where your skill of curiosity becomes valuable. Now, let's delve deeper into each of the five drivers.

1. *I am safe* - We look for safety in all our places and space we occupy - just like our animal ancestors. This applies in our work and personal lives. Our brains are incredible organs, constantly on the lookout and assessing our environment for danger. If there's something we perceive as a threat, we are on guard and ready to fight, flee or freeze! So if employees aren't feeling safe (either physically or psychologically), they are likely to feel and behave defensively.
2. *I matter* - This is about your existence and presence mattering; others notice if you're there or not; that you as a human being matter in this world. This is wired into us. We are social beings with an innate need to be loved and accepted. I encourage you to think of "love" in the work context being about connection and mattering. We can show people at work they are "loved", or that they matter, by showing care and compassion not only for the work they do but for the person they are. We cannot be and do our best in environments where we don't matter. "Remote employees who felt unseen (are) more likely to experience feelings of burnout, loneliness and imposter

syndrome—which translates into feelings of inadequacy and self-doubt—all of which can be detrimental to both employees and their work."[14]

3. *I belong* - People look for and need to feel accepted and part of the team or workplace community. As group/social animals, it's how we survived on this earth! Without belonging to a group or community, we quite simply would die. That drive and need is still within us. Without it our safety is threatened. You can appreciate now how difficult it is then for someone to speak up at work against the norm. It literally threatens their safety. The primitive part of our brain is hard-wired to fit in so we survive, not stand out alone.
4. *My work has meaning* - This is about one's work mattering to someone other than oneself; that it has a purpose that extends beyond oneself, the team, and the company. It's one of the reasons my experience in high tech was so hard as I witnessed project after project get canceled; that after teams of designers worked so hard to meet tight deadlines and project specifications, many times forgoing weekends and evenings with family so they could deliver. The work they contributed had no meaning as it ceased to exist and for some, this was crushing to the point they changed industries in hopes their projects would see the light of day. That said, like the higher level drivers, it too has different value to people. That's why curiosity is your friend so you can ask questions to those on your team - to ***know*** them - and respond appropriately. You can't always control the decision to keep/sideline a project, but knowing your people helps you navigate with confidence and compassion. Don't assume that if it matters to you that it matters to them (and vice versa).

---

[14] Robinson, B., Ph.D. (2022, January 11). 'Mattering' Is The Top Leadership Skill For Retaining Employees, According To Research. *Forbes*. https://www.forbes.com/sites/bryanrobinson/2022/11/01/mattering-is-the-top-leadership-skill-for-retaining-employees-according-to-research/?sh=36522d4076ec

5. *I am growing, learning, and/or achieving* - Virtually everyone has a desire to grow, learn, and/or improve in some form or another. People look to increase competence and get to mastery. Like Driver #4 - my work has meaning - this matters to varying degrees to different people. For example, perhaps one's desire to learn is not in the workplace context but in their personal life. I have a friend who works in the government who is a top performer. She is highly talented, experienced, and skilled. She has assumed short term acting positions countless times to cover vacancies but has declined multiple offers to be promoted. She likes where she is, has no desire to grow upwardly, and likes being the go-to expert. We can't assume. But as leaders, we have a responsibility to inquire and mindfully respond to what emerges.

Applying the Drivers

Know and understand your people. Be curious and genuinely interested. Listen for understanding and insights into who they are and what is important in their lives and work. What matters most to them and why? What are their strengths, preferences, desires and motivators? With this, you have ***information***, instead of your own stories and assumptions, to create and nurture an environment that helps the best in others emerge. This environment and set of factors may connect with them in a way that turns on their own motivation on which they then choose to act on. You can create the fertile ground on which others can then choose to engage, grow, contribute and be productive. This is core to thriving as a leader - you must understand your people.

Abraham Maslow proposed a theory of human motivation in 1943. It's very simple, so powerful and still relevant today. I believe that is why it is so commonly referenced. It's a relatable model that just makes sense. Keep in mind that no model is going to perfectly explain every person and every situation, instead like the *Humanizing Leadership* model, it provides us a mental framework. An explanation of how something works in the surrounding world and the relationship between its various parts. If you're not familiar with *Maslow's Hierarchy of Needs*, he theorized all human beings have needs that can be best understood by looking at them as a hierarchy, which he represents as different levels within a triangle. He asserts that the lower level needs at the base of the triangle are the most basic human needs that are priority needs and that they must be met before the higher level needs are even considered or are deemed important (e.g. unless basic or low level needs like food, water, shelter, sleep are met, you don't care about the higher level needs like accomplishment or fulfilling your potential).

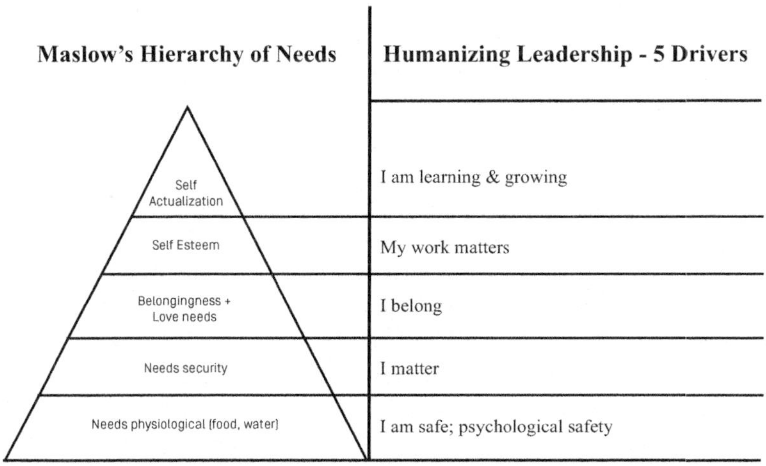

How does this show up in our lives today? All the time, which is why I included an illustration of how Maslow's model shows up at work through the 5 drivers. Take a look at the diagram and consider where in this moment of your life you are on the hierarchy. Then imagine tomorrow disaster hits. It could be a wildfire like we have seen in Australia, California, or Western Canada. Or perhaps take yourself back to March 2020 when COVID first hit. How does that influence where on the hierarchy you are? How do circumstances impact your needs? I think a lot about March 2020 and recall how I immediately went into safety and security mode with the fight-flight-or-freeze in full effect. I felt my body surge with adrenaline, ready to react, stay home, masked, and cocooned. My body reacted with an accelerated heart rate, and my mind was busy sorting out all the details of keeping kids home, getting a home office set up, and figuring out how to order food online for drive by pick up. Mama bear was activated; I was ready for action. It's in each and every one of us ready to be activated in the snap of a finger. In a moment - job loss, death of a loved one, natural disaster - we can get thrown into another level of the hierarchy that we didn't see coming. From pre-COVID-19 concerns of career growth and promotion on the brain to the current reality of worry for our health, safety, livelihood, or even our ability to pay our bills and put food on the table. From level 4 or 5 on Maslow's triangle to level 1 or 2 seemingly overnight. That's Maslow's model in action, relevant still today almost 80 years later. And it has its impact at work, which we have seen.

Consider that there are significant events happening in the lives of our employees that we as leaders may know little about - illness of a family member, personal health issues, mental health challenges. This definitely poses challenges for us, doesn't it? Sadly 95% of people who call in sick for mental health reasons say it's for something else according to a 2017 study from Deloitte Centre for Health Solutions. We are not robots after all and thank goodness for that. Consider for a moment the last time you had a difficult personal experience. Perhaps it was the death or illness of a family member or a close friend, divorce, new baby (oh the sleeplessness!). How did it impact your work, productivity, communication or connection with others? Maybe you were a bit withdrawn, less talkative, less creative, slower to respond to emails. Now consider the *Hierarchy of Needs* – how does this stress or life event impact where you are on the triangle? It doesn't give all the answers but it does create an interesting way of looking at the situation with a little more objectivity, which is missing when we're in our stress brain. Now what about your employees? What may be going on in their lives – personal or work – that impacts their placement on the Hierarchy and affects how they show up to work? What are their motivations and drivers?

You can now start to see and appreciate the nuances in the behaviors of those you lead and how important it is to be connected to your people in order to better understand. You can meet them where they are in their lives, and show up with compassion and well-placed curiosity. This is emotional intelligence and humanizing leadership in action.

The Power of the Pause

We all struggle at different times in our lives for all sorts of reasons, as do your employees. At times we may have done or said things in the heat of the moment (and then regret it later). Through my life and career I've learned the value of what pausing can do. I can hear my mum's voice saying '*think before you speak, Louise.*' I call it the power of the pause.

What do we tell young children who are having a tantrum to help them calm down? We tell them to breathe. What do we encourage people who are nervously waiting for their turn to present in front of a crowd? Take a deep breath, we say. I recall at 12 years old taking a few deep breaths before going on stage at the Kiwanis Music Festival to play my well-rehearsed piano pieces, and much later in life taking a few deep breaths the first time I gave my 16 year old keys to the car when he got his license!

The brief pause and deep breath allows you to slow down and become aware of your inner landscape; your intentions, thoughts and behaviours. The pause and breath helps you get out of the natural defensive, self-focused, tunnel vision perspective and into an others-focused frame of mind. This is the viewpoint where you can understand the motivations and needs of others, building your capacity to create an environment and relationships that foster: caring, compassion, and connection. It's from these relationships and bonds that we can do great work, that we can experiment, innovate, create, fail, try again, and succeed. These relationships create feelings of safety which decrease stress and fear and allow us to fully tap into our thinking brain, which means we get out of protection mode and into the performance zone.

Remember my client who I talked about earlier - the one who thought they needed to improve their strategic thinking but after pausing (and using 1-2-3 Switch) was then able to access the part of their brain where strategic thinking and problem solving took place? Well, the power of the pause helped them in their personal life too. I was on a call with them after their much needed 2 week summer vacation. For months leading up to their vacation, they had been working 60-70 hour weeks and admitted to not really being their best self at home. They were tired, grumpy, and overworked. After the 2 week vacation, like many of us, they returned to work vibrant and refreshed. They told me about how wonderful vacation time had been with their partner and kids. The conversation was punctuated with what came next. They said that after being back to work for only a week, their partner had said "I like the vacation version of you better" Wow - that was direct. And it was also true. They themself liked vacation-self better too. So while they did make some adjustments to their commitments and calendar to re-prioritize work/home, they also implemented the PAUSE before responding to her partner and kids. And with that, not only did their work improve, their marriage did as well.

Lead Your Fear to Feeling

"Leaders must either invest a reasonable amount of time attending to fears and feelings, or squander an unreasonable amount of time trying to manage ineffective and unproductive behavior."

Brené Brown, PhD

Fear; we've all felt it. The rising of panic, sweaty palms and racing heart. The urge to shrink, shirk responsibility, or flee. We know it commonly as the fight or flight response. It's an awful feeling, and for good reason. It's our body's automatic response to keep us safe and alive; to get us to react quickly. It served us well when foraging for food where we had to be vigilant of the sabre-toothed tiger hunting nearby. However, it doesn't serve us well in current day boardrooms when the project we've been working on for 6 months gets challenged, you're feeling overwhelmed in your new job and fear asking your manager for support, or feel stressed and uncertain about an upcoming corporate reorganization.

Fear is a four-letter word we all prefer to ignore, especially in our workplaces. It's hard to acknowledge and navigate our own fears, never mind understand and support others with theirs. If we share our own, we feel vulnerable and exposed for potential ridicule or worse, that it could limit career growth. Yet if we don't, it can affect our relationships, health and how we communicate, perform, and lead at work.

Fear is Human

As human beings, across people and cultures, fear is one of the six universal emotions we experience. It's not a weakness or a fault, in fact to fear is to be human. It's our response to any threat (personal or professional) we may encounter. Our day-to-day realities are filled with what our brains and bodies may perceive as "threats" – long hours, heavy workloads, organizational changes, tight deadlines, job insecurity, industry instability, lack of autonomy, changes to job duties - and therefore our day-to-day realities are also filled with fear. Make no mistake, in this time of unprecedented change, fear is alive and well. The best leaders recognize these fear-based instincts, learn how to navigate them productively, and help others to do the same. The better one does this, the less power one's subconscious human drivers will have.

Putting your head in the sand because you don't know what to do about it, or being like a young child who covers their head with a blanket with the belief "If I can't see it it's not there" may work in the short term. But you're a leader looking beyond the quarterly results; who wishes to achieve those results with the people you lead and not at their expense; and who's willing to dig in, do the work, and say the hard things. A leader who builds people and profits.

3 More Tactics for Humanizing Leadership

Change is the only constant. Change creates uncertainty which often triggers stress or fear. It's our brain's response to the unknown. This means where there is change, there will be fear and stress. It's biology. It's also something we can learn to manage. When we give something a name, when we speak it, we can strategize what to do with it. It transforms the intangibility of stress and fear into tangible action. The *Humanizing Leadership* approach to leading with fear riding side care can be simplified into three steps:

1. *Expect it.* In situations of change, those you lead typically learn of the change far later than you. The higher up the leadership ladder you are, the greater access to information and context you have. You've had time to understand the situation, consider its implications on your work/personal life, and integrate within your own mental model or expectations. Your employees are not where you are. Give them time and space to catch up. They are also different people with a different life, and with a different set of life challenges. They are not you. They are them. Expect different reactions.
2. *Prepare for it.* Preparing to lead self and others through stress, fear and change starts long before any change event itself. When you have a foundation of trust established with those you lead, when you have already done the work, ready yourself for it by working on you first as discussed in Pillar 1 (Lead Self). You can help lead others on your team by building trust, nurturing relationships, and identifying the team's "Positive Core", a term used by Dr. David Cooperrider, to describe the glue that keeps your team strong and whole; the qualities you possess as a team that

will enable you all to navigate periods of change together, intact and strong. The "Positive Core" is something I learned about recently in the exciting and groundbreaking work of "Appreciative Inquiry" as a substantially more successful approach to change than traditional change management approaches. One of the first steps is to identify as a team your "Positive Core" by answering the question "What gives us life?". You'll often hear team values, norms, behaviours and cultural qualities that together embody the essence or spirit of the team.

3. *Communicate.* What's not going to change? In times of change, fear, stress and uncertainty our feeling of safety can be rocked. While employees absolutely need to understand the "why" behind a change, don't lose sight of a vision of the future. Clarify and communicate. It becomes the security blanket individuals and the team can hold onto; that no matter what chaos and ambiguity is happening around them, they can know "This" as something that isn't going to change. In periods of uncertainty, all you may be able to offer is your commitment to the team to remain open and share all you can in a timely fashion. Whatever it is, be sure you can stay true to what you shall maintain. State it often and live it. Be intentional about conveying more positive than negative messages in your communication. More to come on this (and why!) in Chapter 8: Identify Blind Spots.

"F-E-A-R: has two meanings: Forget Everything And Run or Face Everything And Rise. The choice is yours." Zig Ziglar

Choose to Thrive

What are the first words that come out of your mouth or run through your head each workday morning when your alarm goes off? "Morning already?" Or "is it Friday yet?" Or "I can't handle another day at the office?"

I attended a Tony Robbins event in 2018 and one of the speakers was this 80 something year old spit fire of a woman, Loretta LaRoche. She had superbly combined her gift of humor with her over 30 years of experience in stress management. My biggest takeaway was something I still use today, every single morning in fact. She asked the audience - what would happen if each morning when you awoke, you sat up, threw your arms in the air and exclaimed: "I'm back!" instead of the other thoughts that drag you down and make you feel miserable. Since that day, every morning when my partner brings me my coffee I do just that. I sit up, throw my arms in the air and exclaim "I'm back!". Some days I say it with a chuckle and vigor, other days admittedly require a little more mental fortitude, but each day it puts a smile on my face and starts my day off right. Coupled with the thought: "I ***get*** to go to work today," (instead of "I ***have*** to") my days started off brighter. With each new dawn comes great possibilities. Small mindset shifts and little actions taken daily add up to significant transformation in life and work. They do for me, and they can for you too.

Optimism for Flourishing

Great leaders face life with hope, envision an inspired future, and compel others to join them on the journey. They are grounded in reality ***and*** are optimistic about the future. Not only do optimists live longer, there's neuroscience that speaks to its many benefits. "...every thought releases brain chemicals. Being focused on negative thoughts effectively saps the brain of its positive forcefulness, slows it down, and can go as far as dimming your brain's ability to function, even creating depression. On the flip side, thinking positive, happy, hopeful, optimistic, joyful thoughts decrease cortisol and produce serotonin, which creates a sense of well-being. This helps your brain function at peak capacity." Is it a cure-all? Of course not. But creating and maintaining a positive (not naive) and optimistic outlook is part of what it takes to be an effective leader that leaves a legacy; not merely the leader who achieves the numbers for the quarter.

Optimism builds self and others up and is an inner force that helps drive us forward in the face of obstacles.

When we are bombarded with messages all day long, many of them negative, we have a choice whether to feed the negativity further or flip the script and choose optimism, hope and positivity. Humanized leaders intentionally accept this as their responsibility, not unknowingly bear it as a burden.

"Human Flourishing", as researched extensively by Dr. Martin Seligman (founder of Positive Psychology) describes the elements that contribute to a life well lived, a life of both success and fulfillment. To bring Seligman's model to life I envision a tree to represent us as human beings. Under the ground are the tree's extensive root system which nourishes and stabilizes the tree. There is no tree health without root health. And yet, that is all taking place below the ground, not visible to us. I see the leaves/fruit of the tree as our accomplishments – what we and others objectively observe – the fruits of our labor so to speak. What we don't see is the work, focus, self-care/health practices, help of others, "blood, sweat and tears", etc. that went into realizing these accomplishments. We don't see these behind the scenes activities that contributed to these accomplishments; activities which enabled the tree to bear fruit. We don't see the support of others (relationships), the personal commitment to health, the flow one gets into when doing this work that brings meaning, etc. The point is that without nurturing our own roots, like the tree, we will not have sustained brilliance. We will not be able to weather the seasons and storms of life without a strong root system. As a leader this is critical to leading self. You need to be strong in ***yourself*** so you can be of service to others, inspire a shared vision, and empower others to join the journey.

Seligman has found in his work over the last 30 plus years that a well-lived life isn't the absence of misery but instead the presence of 5 things, known as the PERMA-H model:

1. ***P**ositive emotions* - This refers to the presence of feelings like joy, comfort, happiness, being merry and cheerful. Yes, there are genetics at play here, but there is also evidence that you can cultivate more joy. Note that this is 1/6 of Seligman's model, so don't assume positive psychology is only the happy, fluffy stuff! Consider for a moment the play that's instinctual in mammals. One of my favourite times to visit the zoo is in the spring when new babies are born. Seeing the play instinct alive and well brings me so much joy! Would you like to consistently find joy in your life? Think back to something that lit you up when you were young. Explore this memory. If you didn't have a hobby, try something new now. You may be pleasantly surprised by what you find.
2. ***E**ngagement* - . Some of us may know this as "flow" or the feeling of being lost in a task that you don't even notice the passage of time, you may miss meals, and not even go to the washroom. You're so in tune with what you're doing, you simply lose yourself in it. It occurs when your greatest strengths match your highest challenges. Mindfulness, the act of being in the present moment that we talked about in Practice 1 makes us flow-ready.

3. ***R**elationships* - Good relationships, that is! This is a skill. There have been discoveries that show that we can teach/ learn good relationship skills if it isn't something that comes naturally, and that it is fundamental to our wellbeing.
4. ***M**eaning* - Belonging to and serving towards something bigger than oneself; the notion that individuality doesn't fuel us, in fact it harms us. Turns out we are hive creatures like wasps and bees!
5. ***A**chievement* - Accomplishment, mastery, competence. This is best known to us in our high-achieving, type-A culture. This is when we set and achieve goals, learn a new concept, practice and master it; when we work so hard at something we become an expert in our domain. This is achievement.
6. ***H**ealth* - It almost goes without saying that attention to our health - mental, physical, emotional, and spiritual - is essential to our wellbeing. What we often don't do is recognize its connection to our ability to achieve our goals.

Integrating the old (Maslow's Hierarchy of Needs) with the new (Seligman's PERMA-H model), the 5 Drivers simplify a leader's approach to getting to know and engaging others in a way that matters to them. No need to try different strategies to engage your employees (e.g. assuming it's a promotion or salary increase they want), which is akin to throwing spaghetti at the wall to see what will stick. Instead use the 5 drivers as a tool of inquiry openly with those on your team. Share with them what you're doing and why you're asking the questions you are. Not only will it serve to strengthen the relationship between you and those you lead, but it will also increase their sense of personal agency, and help build the next generation of humanized leaders.

CHAPTER FIVE

Unleash the Power of Your People

> *As we look ahead into the next century, leaders will be those who empower others. — Bill Gates*

Those who empower leave others better equipped, confident, and capable of leading themselves, making decisions and taking aligned action; that under your leadership they have grown as a person and as a professional.

In our quest to be better leaders and to do so swiftly, many well-intentioned leaders/aspiring leaders start here – empowering others – without first doing the inner work to be able to empower others successfully. Consider the analogy of teaching someone to swim. A qualified swimming instructor does not throw a non-swimmer into the deep end to figure it out on their own; "sink or swim". Instead there are some fundamental principles, skills and techniques they first teach: comfort in the shallow end of the pool, blowing bubbles, getting face wet, floating, kicking, etc. Likewise, with great leadership, there are critical skills that need to be learned before you can effectively and authentically bring out the best in others. Some of us naturally develop some of these skills over time, depending on our personality, experiences and preferences, but other skills have to be learned, practiced and honed. Whatever way you get to them - through nature or nurture - if you're a leader, get to them!

"Our job is obvious: We need to get out of the way, shine a light, and empower a new generation to teach itself and to go further and faster than any generation ever has."

Seth Godin

Have you ever considered what happens between an employee's first day and the day they hand in their resignation? From day one: full of passion, ready to learn, and eager to be productive; to the day that same employee hands in their notice of resignation? What happened in between those two points in time? Think about the last job you resigned from. Why did you accept that job in the first place? What was the appeal? How did you feel on your first day? As the days, weeks, months and years passed, what changed? What happened that led to your ultimate resignation?

There have been many studies on employee engagement and leadership and much research continues now in our post-pandemic reality. There have been many employee engagement surveys completed and analyzed, many exit interviews conducted. Gallup's meta-analysis, which includes decades worth of data, shows that "...high engagement - largely defined as having a strong connection with one's work and colleagues, feeling like a real contributor, and enjoying ample changes to learn - consistently leads to positive outcomes for both individuals and organizations."[15] Furthermore, the Deloitte Millennial Survey (2018) suggests Millennials and the generation that follows (Gen Z) will not be hanging around any of our workplaces all that long. Turns out they don't trust their leaders (and who can blame them with all the corporate scandals and social media "outings"?), nor are they satisfied with training and development opportunities. They are leaving their organizations to keep their skills and marketability current. This demographic also wants our organizations to come out of the Dark Ages and into modern-

[15] Zak, P. J. (2017, January 1). The Neuroscience of Trust. *Harvard Business Review*. https://hbr.org/2017/01/the-neuroscience-of-trust

day as it relates to work environments, workplace flexibility, and diversity. And the number 1 reason people quit their jobs? Inability to learn and grow that in fact it's easier to do so outside the organization they are in![16]

Do we really need research and reports to tell us this? Don't get me wrong - I appreciate and value research and data; but as individual leaders, we have so much "data" already at our fingertips, if we only took a moment of pause with a desire to see it, and then act accordingly with it. For leaders, it comes down to one simple question: How can I give people a reason to stay instead of a reason to quit?

Let's go back to the day one experience of a new hire. Here you have a person you've spent hours of your time recruiting, interviewing, and finally selecting. It's a long process and requires an investment of time and money. Assuming you hired well, you have a motivated person in front of you with the right combination of knowledge, skills, abilities and other attributes to do well in this job position. What comes next is largely up to you - the leader. And if I may be blunt, this is where leaders fail miserably. Yes, my friends - some of you as early as day one. How, you may ask? I see many leaders not there on day one to greet and welcome the new hire. The number of leaders who have rushed to hire; turned the arms of IT and HR to get the new hire started faster, only to be on vacation or otherwise unavailable for the new hire start date. Others haven't planned sufficiently for the new hire's arrival and just wing it or pass the new hire off to another member of the team who's surprised, albeit willing to help, but equally unprepared to onboard them. Email accounts have not been set up, access to software and systems needed for the new hire to be successful in the role have not been established. All this because of the pressure you put on internal teams to force a "quick-hire". Expectations aren't clear about what success looks like for the end of: week 1, week 2, month 1, month 3, etc.

---

[16] Greenwood, E. R. (n.d.). *Workers are leaving. What can you do about it?* Deloitte. Insights2Action. https://action.deloitte.com/insight/2737/workers-are-leaving.-what-can-you-do-about-it

Organizations with a strong onboarding process improve new hire retention by 82% and productivity by over 70% (Glassdoor, 2015).

The truth is, when we show up in alignment with our values and vision, have awareness of our own mindset and emotions (hello "1-2-3 Switch"), and approach our people with compassion, curiosity, and with the Platinum Rule, we can figure out a lot of this on our own! Look, listen and feel your way to identify where your employees are and meet them there. Their behaviour is bound to be driven by the need for one, or some combination, of these needs:.

- I am safe.
- I matter.
- I belong.
- My work has meaning.
- I am growing and learning.

Play Your Position

Leaders, like everyone in the organization, have a role or position to play. Are you clear on what yours is and how to play it? Do your employees know theirs? Do you all know each other's?

Whether you are a sports fan or not, it's fair to say that most of us know that professional athletes each have a position that they play in their chosen sport. There are coaches and other support staff (physiotherapists, chiropractors, trainers, etc.), all with an area of expertise, critical for the functioning of the team. Working together is how they maximize individual and collective effectiveness. It's how they win championships. We never see the irate basketball coach who is tearing up and down the sidelines of a game sub in for one of their players because a player on the court isn't playing well, *do we?* Or a soccer coach decides they will take their place in net instead of the goalie because they have let too many goals in and they think they can do a better job. Of course not. In fact, it seems laughable or like a ridiculous analogy. And yet I see this happening all the time in the workplace.

Players in sports know their role. They know what they are accountable for. They know where to go and when; and they know how to support their teammates. Each member of the team knows their role, what's expected of them in training and on Game Day. What happens when they don't? They eventually get traded.

Evaluate your leadership role by answering these questions:

- What's your position?
- Are you clear on your position's purpose?
- What are your most important accountabilities?
- What are you uniquely positioned to action and see through to completion?
- Are you clear on the decisions you are meant to own, influence and/or have veto power over?

Clarity is paramount! Get clear on your role and give clarity to those on your team. I have seen many frustrated leaders wanting their employees to step up and take responsibility and make decisions but weren't doing it themselves. They weren't modeling the way. Before you point the finger, hold up the mirror to ensure you're fulfilling your responsibilities and accountabilities. Experience tells me leaders who lack this clarity in their own role have employees who lack the same clarity.

If you're one of those people or leaders who believe that "Leadership would be great if it wasn't for people", (I've heard that before - honestly!) please find another line of work. The success and wellbeing of people is in your hands. The best leaders I've had are ones who know and play their roles; and support their employees in playing theirs.

While this concept of role clarity and playing your own position isn't a new function of good leadership, its importance and impact have intensified in our increasingly volatile, complex and ambiguous business reality. We're all being asked to do more, with less, and do it faster. We can't possibly do it successfully alone. We need to rely on those we hire and work alongside; to do the thing they were hired to do, so we can do what we were hired to do! What are you uniquely positioned to do? Do more of that! It avoids confusion and frustration, helps to readily identify overlaps and gaps in roles within our ever-changing, ever-evolving business realities. Just as importantly, role expectations and role clarity have a significant hand in maintaining your employees' mental wellbeing. It was so critical that in 2013 Canada launched The National Standard of Canada for Psychological Health and Safety in the Workplace (the Standard) – the first of its kind in the world. It is a set of guidelines, tools and resources intended to guide organizations in promoting mental health and preventing psychological harm at work. This standard identified "clear leadership and expectations" as a workplace factor affecting psychological health and safety. Considering our rising rates of mental health challenges and its impact on the human experience and on bottom line results; role clarity and expectations are not "nice to have" my friends. It is a key responsibility of leadership, it's table stakes. *Humanizing Leadership* recognizes the importance and impact of having clear role expectations on mental health. How? It starts with you.

Know your own responsibilities and decision-making bounds first. Once you're clear, you'll be able to make it very clear to others ***what*** you want, ***when*** you want it, and ***who*** needs to be involved. If you tend to be non-specific in your expectations of your employees, why is that? Is it because you don't know what your expectations really are? Or you just haven't told them?

One of my former managers made it very clear to her direct reports that she expected us to manage up. She let it be known in a kind and direct manner that if we were missing information or clarity, it was our responsibility to ask for it. This reduced ambiguity because if there was any, we asked. Remember that your employees are adults - treat them as such! Yes, it's your responsibility to be clear in what you ask for, and it's also your employees' responsibility to ask for guidance when they are unclear or lack information. Being clear involves:

- What - What's the task/project?
- Why - Why is it important? Why is the task/project being done in the first place?
- When - When is it due? Are there important milestone dates along the way? And when do you as the leader expect updates?
- Who - Who needs to be involved? What are their roles? Who is making the decisions? Who needs to be consulted for input?
- How - How does this project/task need to be done? ***Leave this part up to your people.*** This is why you hired them! Those doing the work are often the best ones to figure out the best way to get it done. Remain available if needed and give them the freedom to do what they were hired to do.

The kind of leader who does this well requires self-awareness of their skills and areas of expertise along with the confidence to be able to admit when they don't know or have not got the answers; has the network to be able to connect employees with others (internal and external to the organization) to help employees get what they need; and doesn't let fear, ego or control creep in because timelines slip or the project gets off track.

Too simple? It really is and yet so rarely done well. This approach, one that we already know, is powerful when consistently applied. It allows you to play your position, your employees to play theirs, and is effective delegation in action. If we want A-players on our teams, "The best of the best" and out of the box thinkers; your leadership must match that. You must be the A-player leader, "The best of the best", and an out of box leader. Are you?

The Magic of Being in the Zone

Have you ever been so focused and engaged in a task or project that you don't notice the passage of time? You were likely working on something that was both challenging yet doable. While engrossed in the activity, you likely didn't pause to eat, drink or even use the washroom; time seemed to stand still. This state is what Prof. Mihaly Csikszentmihalyi, a psychologist best known for his work in positive psychology, has labeled flow, which he described as "Being completely involved in an activity for its own sake. The ***ego*** falls away. Time flies. Every action, movement, and thought follows inevitably from the previous one, like playing jazz. Your whole being is involved, and you're using your skills to the utmost." When in this state it can be a great way to achieve your goals, to be productive and nurture wellbeing.

Think about a time when you were in "the zone" or a flow state. What were you doing? Likely something that you enjoyed or were curious/learning about. Something that gave you energized focus and enjoyment. Have you ever felt like that at work? I have. And since that time in my life where I was forced to reconsider my life choices and choose a different path, it's been full of flow. The impacts of working in this state have been far reaching. My relationships are deeper, my perspective on life more joyful, and the work I'm doing with clients has greater personal meaning. Not until this point in my life had I said: "I'm richer than I've ever been in my life despite what my bank account says". Yet in order to use my strengths more fully to experience this personal and professional transformation and state of flow, I had to create it for myself. I had to venture out on my own; to start my own business and life as a coach, leadership development consultant, and writer. And I'm so glad I did. I've been able to experience firsthand what Csikszentmihalyi's research said, which is: flow can both improve performance and enhance personal wellbeing.

"The best moments in our lives are not the passive, receptive, relaxing times . . . The best moments usually occur if a person's body or mind is stretched to its limits in a voluntary effort to accomplish something difficult and worthwhile" (Csikszentmihalyi, 1990).

It's not just me who has been positively impacted by this concept of "Flow". In fact, many well-known successful people have been influenced by Csikszentmihalyi and his book *Flow: The Psychology of Optimal Experience.* What if you as a leader could create more "Flow" for those you lead? What impact could that have on your people, their fulfillment, their engagement and their output? I see no losers in this equation. Dr. Martin Seligman talks about the importance of flow, which is essentially Engagement in his *Human Flourishing* model. He states: *"Pleasure is the least consequential... engagement and meaning are much more important."* Considering how much of our lives we spend at work, it makes sense for us to pursue (and hire people into) roles that excite and engage. It's core to a life well lived. It's one of the roots of a flourishing life. You owe it to yourself to do more of this type of work and you owe it to your employees to create and nurture an environment that allows for greater flow. There's no loser!

"Surveys and scientific studies have found that while most people enjoy working when it provides Flow, too few jobs are designed to make Flow possible."[17] So here's your challenge. What can you do better now with this knowledge of the importance and impact of flow, both for yourself and for those you lead?

[17] Bakker, A.B., van Woerkom, M. Flow at Work: a Self-Determination Perspective. *Occup Health Sci* 1, 47–65 (2017). https://doi.org/10.1007/s41542-017-0003-3

Use Strengths to Transform

In a time of great flow, one is likely using their strengths. When I'm in flow, I'm connecting with others - teaching, writing, coaching, or sharing knowledge with others in a way that equips them to take action in their own lives. This, I've come to learn, is because I'm using my strengths of Activator, Relator, Learner, Input, and Individualization (CliftonStrengths). In short, this means that I'm at my best when I:

- make things happen by turning thoughts into action,
- nurture close relationships while working towards achieving a goal,
- learn, learn, learn simply for the enjoyment of learning,
- work closely with others to unlock their unique qualities (at an individual and team level).

Research done by Gallup has found that when we use our strengths more often than not, and learn to navigate our lesser strengths, we are set up to live our strongest possible life and reach our potential. As a leader, you should care deeply about this. It's a key to both helping your employees BE their best and also GET their best. The data shows links to higher engagement, better performance, and decreased risk of turnover. It turns out that playing more to our strengths and managing, navigating or mitigating our weaker areas serves us, our employees and our organization's bottom lines and lives better.

Once again, bring to mind the time when you felt a sense of great Flow. What strengths of yours were you utilizing? How can you use this awareness of Flow and strengths to ensure those you lead use their strengths more often, supporting the opportunity for greater moments of Flow to enhance performance? "The task of leadership is to create an alignment of strengths in ways that make weaknesses irrelevant." Peter Drucker

Strengths actually do more than perform; they transform. Leading change is all about leveraging them. The 2019 Deloitte Human Capital Trends report indicates that one of the best predictors of high engagement is the answer to the question: *"How often do I get to use my strengths at work?"* Gervase R. Bushe, Ph.D. suggests leaders ask questions such as:

- Do we understand why people come to work each day?
- When do they bring the best of themselves and care about the company's results?

- What do we do to make it more likely that people who work here will have new ideas and act on the good ones?

Have you ever considered these questions personally or for those you lead? Where someone works - remote, hybrid, in the office - these all apply. This is, in part, how we'll end "human cubicle suffering" and this is your role as a humanized leader. There is an incredible strengths-based, positive change revolution occurring in the psychology and management sciences fields. It has its foundation in social work and the wellbeing of our people; with the mission of our companies thriving being a significant outcome. Gallup Clifton Strengths research is clear, wide and deep and shows us how bringing out the best in others by igniting their core character strengths is worth the effort:

- 6x more likely to be engaged at work;
- 7.8% more productive in their role; and
- 3x more likely to have a higher quality of life.

When I've had jobs where most of my time was spent using my strengths, I found myself waking up with a volunteer vs. prisoner attitude. Volunteers CHOOSE their work, prisoners don't. What would employee productivity and personal wellbeing be if we all woke up each morning with the attitude: " I ***get*** to go to work today" (volunteer) instead of "I ***have*** to go to work today" (prisoner)?

Your Team & Their Strengths

With curiosity and a few simple steps, you can recognize and acknowledge the strengths of those you lead and seek to craft opportunities that will grow them in areas where they naturally excel. Humanized leaders see in others what they don't see in themselves, you seek to reveal and explore them. If you've not engaged in this type of personal exploration yourself, try it. You may be surprised at what you learn.

1. Ask others - Ask a few trusted friends and/or colleagues to name three strengths they've noticed or observed. How and when did they see those strengths demonstrated?

2. Take a strengths survey (e.g. CliftonStrengths through Gallup) - For less than $75 you can gain invaluable insight into your top strengths and how to better put them to use, as well as your lesser strengths and now to navigate them. Awareness into my strengths and lesser strengths, has transformed how I design, do, and delegate work. When doing work that requires me to use my lesser strengths (like focus and discipline to get projects across the finish line) I've learned it will take more deliberate attention and energy. This often means using my strengths of relationship building and relating with others to collaborate or delegate work and projects that are not aligned with these strengths. In contrast, when I'm engaged in work around my core strengths, coaching leaders, delivering leadership training, and workshop facilitation, I can access them with ease. On a practical level this means, when possible, I schedule work that requires my lesser strengths when I know I have more time/energy. I time block and time-bound this work to help create a sense of urgency of "getting it done" so I don't get

too depleted. Through experience, I've learned to avoid or limit, scheduling a full day that requires my lesser strengths because it's a recipe for an exhausted, disengaged Louise. Gaining this level of insight into my strengths has enabled me to take more charge over my energy, how I show up for others effectively, and clarity on how to perform at my best. How might this type of awareness change the work you engage in? How you hire or onboard new members to your team? How you engage your current employees in career conversations?

3. Self-Reflect - Figure out what tasks and activities you regularly do that ***strengthen*** you and ***weaken*** you? For example, I took a piece of paper and drew a vertical line down the centre of the page. On one side of the vertical line at the top of the page I wrote "love". On the other side of the vertical line I wrote "loathe". I carried this sheet with me everywhere for a week. When I engaged in a task or activity that activated a feeling of "love" or "loathe", I recorded it in real-time, in the appropriate column. At the end of the week it was quite revealing and telling.I tallied how much of my time was spent doing work or engaging in non-work activities that I loathed vs. loved and it was clear something had to change. It too was one of the clarity exercises I completed during my transition from full time HR leader to entrepreneur, business owner, coach, leadership development consultant and writer. Reflection is a powerful tool to gain greater awareness to be able to make positive changes in one's life.

When you do this, and explore it with your employees, you'll have insights, awareness and knowledge you hadn't previously had. And knowledge is power. Knowing you would be more productive and fulfilled if you spent more of your day doing work/activities that strengthened you as opposed to weakened you, consider the following questions:

- What internal mindset is holding you back from using your strengths more often?
- How can you in the context of your current role put your strengths to greater use?
- How can you leverage your strengths more to benefit your employer, your career, and your overall wellbeing?
- How are you able to adjust your work to do more of what you love and less of what you loathe?

Once your employees have answered the same questions as you did above, consider if there are other ways to organize and/or redistribute the workload to create greater opportunity for flow in your team. As a humanized leader you have the ability to help them identify, explore and better use their strengths. You'll be amazed what possibilities are revealed when you get out of the Clouds of Chaos and Stress (fight or flight) and into the Sea of Calm (rest and digest). Your perspective will widen, your curiosity deepen, and leadership elevate. ***This*** is *Humanizing Leadership* in action!

Be the Change

Although you may not be able to control all the changes your organization undergoes, you can control your response to it; and as an individual and leader be a positive force for change. How can you be that lightning rod of hope and positivity for those you lead without being too "out there" that people don't believe you, and yet inspiring enough that others follow your mission?

3 Steps to Create Collective Change:

1. Create a compelling vision of the future - Invite your employees to help you paint it. What are examples of what's gone well in the company? Use those stories and images to create that future vision. Hold onto that positive

core that gets unearthed through employee conversation. That positive core is what unites the team and will be deeply tied to employees' own values (and hopefully the organization's values too!). Use the personal stories and experiences to bring your positive vision to life in a way that engages the hearts and minds of your people.

2. Clarify what isn't going to change - There may not be much you can hold onto; but if your will is active, you can find something. State it. Again. And again. And again. It becomes a security blanket that employees can hold onto; a grounding truth to help create a sense of safety and team connection while so much else is changing around them. It acts as a basecamp.

3. Maintain a good positive to negative ratio in your communications - We are wired to pay attention to, seek out, and hold onto the negative events, emotions, and experiences. (We talk more about this in Chapter 8, Identify Blind Spots). Knowing that this tendency is simply being human, it makes sense why sharing positive messages or updates don't have the staying power or stickiness that negative messages and experiences have. You know this now, so do better at finding and sharing the great work that's going on. Reward and recognize outcomes ***and*** effort, teamwork, and other behaviours related to success, company values, and the positive core. As Dr. Martin Seligman has found in his research: curing the negatives does not create the positives. Get in the habit of starting your own staff meetings with "What's gone well?" and train your own leaders to find the positive too for their leadership meetings and events. It's not fake positivity, it's good leadership.

CHAPTER SIX

Dispel Myths that Limit Leaders

> *When we breakaway from the myths of our culture, we stimulate new thought and leadership.*
>
> *When we break through our cultural myths, a whole new reality becomes possible.*

Myth is defined as a widely held but false belief or idea. When I googled the phrase "leadership myths" it rendered 40,200,000 results! That's a lot of myth, misinformation and misunderstanding. Where does all this myth come from? Well, we are full of knowledge, opinions and perspectives – some of which help our leadership, others that hinder. As we go through life we learn from a variety of sources –parents, family members, educators, books, school studies, peers, social media, culture, religion, world events, life experiences, colleagues, etc. From all of these we develop a world view – ***our*** world view – which we bring with us into all the roles we play in our lives, including our leadership. Along the way, we'll have learned truths and some untruths, or myths, which we hold as fact. This is a common and normal human experience, not one to be judged but instead understood so they don't hinder our ability to make decisions and lead others. In this Pillar we'll explore 3 common leadership myths, why they limit leaders, and how to overcome them.

In researching for *Humanizing Leadership*, I was challenged by my coach to come up with 100 leadership myths of my own. The three I chose to focus on in this chapter are those that I don't see getting enough airtime in leadership discussions yet are myths that I observe having considerable impact on leaders and their effectiveness: The Myth of Always On, The Myth of Multitasking, and The Myth of Vulnerability.

The Myth of Always On

Myth: The more I do and the faster I go, the more I'll achieve. Busy = productive.

Truth: When we slow down, pace ourselves, and are intentional about what gets our attention, we achieve more.

We are drowning. Our to-do lists are endless. We take too few breaks and view downtime as a form of weakness. Everyone I know is busy, playing catch up, even feeling anxious and guilty when they aren't juggling many balls at the same time. In an era of increasing work demands, "life" pressure, and 24-7 connectivity we are killing our productivity, relationships, health and bottom lines with this addiction to "busy". We have likely experienced this state ourselves and if we are honest, know this state of busy or "always on", often doesn't equate to productivity and/or wellbeing. And despite working at a detrimental pace, many leaders and their employees continue in this manner. We have not stopped to review why we glorify busy. And yet we have a choice: you can change the pace or the pace will change you for the worse.

Busyness Syndrome. It simply means "having a great deal to do". It quickly turns from something we do; to something we are—a psychological state. I see it in the workplace daily. Running from meeting to meeting (virtual or in-person), no time for washroom breaks or lunch. One meeting ends at the top of the hour and at the exact same moment, the next one starts. "Beam me up Scotty!" comes to mind. I worked with a senior leader who admitted to me that he doesn't drink anything all day so that he doesn't have to use the washroom throughout the workday – that there isn't enough time. It's ridiculous! Pause for a moment to consider the race and pace we are living day in and day out. What race are you running? Where is the finish line? Is there one? If there is, what happens when/if you get there?

In a recent conversation I had with a VP of HR I asked: "While many of us acknowledge we are running a marathon at a sprint pace, has anyone considered that we're not in a race? That instead **we're on a journey with no finish line**?" We need this longer-term perspective in mind if we are going to successfully consider wellbeing, sustainability, and longer term viability.

I know you're looking to deliver value and develop people, that you've either personally experienced the negative effects of busyness or witnessed the impact it's had on others, and you're eager to try alternate approaches. I invite you to start by reflecting on how you and your team members allocate and make use of your time. Because guess what state our brain is in when we're racing through life in our busy, "always on" reality? You guessed it – the stressed out, sympathetic, fight, flight, freeze state. And we already know that there's no thinking, empathy, or innovation going on there, instead there's reacting, surviving, and putting out fires.

Here are a few examples of approaches I've seen organizations experiment with in attempts to carve out and preserve desk/thinking time. Keep in mind that not every example would work in every organization however, you don't have to get an experiment right, right?

- "No meeting Wednesdays"
- Meetings may only be booked between certain hours of the day, for example only 9am to noon and 1pm to 4pm
- Using automation in outlook. For example, the default time allotment for a 1 hour meeting is set for 50 minutes. Enable tech to help us start and maintain these healthier habits. In this space between meetings there's

time to breathe, break, synthesize what just happened in the meeting or take a moment to prepare for the next flurry of activity.

- No meetings on Mondays until 11am to provide employees with time to transition to thinking about work, focus and plan their day and week ahead.

Thinking time; space in between to simply be, reflect, rest, and/or integrate is invaluable in our quest to problem solve, innovate, and collaborate. This time becomes sacred. Consider again the "1-2-3- Switch" technique. If you don't want the stress brain driving the bus (you're the bus by the way) then switch who's driving the bus through conscious breathing.

So, if being busy is so bad, why do we do it?

10 Reasons Why We Choose to Be Busy (and why it's a bad idea!)

Busy makes us...	
+ 😁	- 😨
• Feel smart • Feel important • Feel relevant • Feel worthy • Feel productive • Feel valuable • Feel accomplished • Appear successful	• Unfocussed • Stressed • Overwhelmed & frantic • Mentally & physically unhealthy • Less innovative & creative • Disconnected from others • Less productive • Depressed & anxious • Burned out

Say "No" To Busy

Busyness is a choice. I said it! You may get irritated at this statement, wondering how on earth all the things on your busy to-do list are a choice – getting kids up and ready in the morning, getting yourself ready for work, doing dog duty and/ or childcare drop off and pick up, putting in a productive day at work, doing the dinner-homework-activity-family routine (you get the picture). The COVID-19 pandemic has taught us many things, including what a busy existence we have normalized in developed countries, certainly in Canada and the United States. When we were ***forced*** to pause, some people who had the privilege to do so, used it as an opportunity for introspection. In that introspection I witnessed people seeing for the first time their role in (co)creating their busy, chaotic, and non-stop schedule. Some people I know made some massive shifts in their lives since then with the intention of building more living (instead of doing) into their daily lives. You see, once we recognize the busy paradigm we have built our lives within, we can choose other. How we see our inner world drives everything – every aspect of how we love, live, lead, parent. While simple in concept, I realize this is not easily applied; especially considering the North American context. It's a mental shift that requires intention, vigilance, and discipline as we learn a new way, a more aligned, productive, and joyful way of being ourselves in this world; of achieving success and building a fulfilling life in a way that has less stress, more presence of mind, and greater impact.

How to Banish Busy to Pump Up Productivity and Wellbeing

Stress is literally killing us. *How much more data and evidence do we need before we choose to do something about it?* The busyness mindset is taking us off course in life, and as a leader, you have a responsibility to help steer and best guide those within your sphere of influence. This starts with you and being the example, going first, showing the way and encouraging others to follow suit. Consider for example what you say "no" to, how you prioritize, how you support your team to prioritize the 'important' from the 'busy' work so that being busy is rare and not the norm. This is hard. But with burnout, mental health concerns, turnover, etc. being what it is, what choice do we have? This never was sustainable. We've been pushed to the edge. And it's time to do something about it.

I offer you three simple steps, ones that are simple conceptually but not easy to operationalize: shift your mindset, manage your emotions, and master your time. These require intention and attention; discipline and consistency. The benefits are significant and your health, family, and team at work will thank you for it as your productivity increases joyfully! You'll also improve your ability to form and maintain relationships, make decisions that enhance performance, and free up time for the important work you're uniquely positioned to do. Let's dig in!

STEP 1: Shift your Mindset

Swap the busyness mindset for a growth mindset; a mental model of lack to one of possibilities. Stop the glorification of busy and wearing busy like a badge of honour. For example, drop the label "Supermom" for working mothers who appear to have it all together while juggling "all the things". It's unrealistic and harmful, whether you use it to describe others or an ideal you aspire to. It puts undue pressure and expectations on professional/working moms, perpetuating that busyness is what we should be striving for. Let's consider the impact this is having on the "listening ears" in our homes – our children - and those at work watching the example we set. Perhaps these busy working parents are one comment away from their "house of cards" falling to the ground. Instead, when we can see or sense that others are overloaded, let's ask how we can help. And then actually do something to help. Why is it that the folks who pull the all-nighters a couple of weeks leading up to a deadline get recognized or the hero that comes in at the final hour gets all the glory? What would it look like if instead we rewarded consistent performers who plan well, achieve consistently, and manage their time and themselves in a more steady output. Not sexy or not dramatic. But efficient, effective, and productive, and sustainable. This style is not typically noticed or rewarded as much, but shouldn't it be? Let's make it so!

STEP 2: Manage your thoughts and emotions, don't let them manage you

Once again, the "1-2-3- Switch" technique works here. Unhijack your nervous system and let the blood flow to the thinking part of your brain. It's there that you connect with your values, and are better able to think strategically, listen (*really* listen) to others, and solve problems. From this place of calm you can ask: 'What's the next right thing to do?' When situations (especially the tough ones) are approached this way, you will consistently be making informed, well thought out decisions and taking the best action towards achieving your most important goals. This is where you'll find and unleash the 4 Cs of leadership: character, courage, compassion and curiosity.

STEP 3: Master your time

How does taking control of your day sound to you? It's simple in concept, but hard in practice because it requires focus, commitment, and discipline. Yes there's a lot to do. What's also true is you can't create more hours in a day. The most successful people are in charge of their day by developing habits of intention and attention. There are books and courses dedicated to this topic of time management because many of us struggle with it, but allow me to share a simple approach that when applied with consistency and discipline works wonders.

"The secret of being productive lies in choosing what to do — and doing it right — instead of mindlessly doing more and more on autopilot."

Gustavo Razzetti.

I like simple. And so does the human brain. We like chunks that build on each other, like lego, and that describes my "Plan-Do-Reflect" approach. While the details of what works for me may not work for you in exactly the same way, what matters is that you find a few techniques that do work; techniques that maximize your day, your energy, and your productivity. And then be diligent and disciplined in showing up consistently. That's how we build healthy habits and what the habits of ***intention*** and ***attention*** are all about. I equate forming good habits to a healthy financial investment strategy; that when done intentionally and consistently over time, you reap rewards for years.

a) ***Plan*** Your Day - Establish a good routine for how you start and end your day, no matter how short. Science tells us why it's a smart thing to do. You see, our brains cling to certainty, familiarity and routine. This means that creating and sticking to a routine that sets you up to achieve your goals increases your chances of reaching them. How do you normally start your days? What does your morning routine look like? I know when my children were young, weekday mornings were a blur. They were a flurry of getting myself ready, making lunches, dressing the boys, school and daycare drop off, and rushing to get to the office hoping to be in clothes that didn't have crusty food residue from breakfast. If I knew then what I know now, I would have gotten up before kids rose – even 15 minutes earlier – to start my day with intention, with a sense of groundedness and personal control. During and since the COVID-19 pandemic, many of us had our morning and end-of-day routines abruptly changed. My favourite strategy for those work-from-home days? Recreate the commute! Go for a walk, meditate, do yoga, read a book…just do *something* routinely to signal to your brain you're transitioning to/from work. The consequence of not? We fill that time with other "to-do's" and we create more busyness in our lives, more stress, and further disconnect from ourselves which in the long run helps no one. Here's more insight into how I plan my days; strategies that together keep me grounded, focused, and moving forward towards my most important work (without losing sight of the joys along the way). These sound simple, but it's taken me years experimenting with different approaches to find what works for me.

- The Week at a Glance: For me "Plan" starts every Sunday evening. I sit in my favourite comfy chair with my pen-and-paper agenda alongside my electronic calendar in my hand. In the winter I'll have my cozy throw and cup of tea close by. I make it a quick yet enjoyable part of my Sunday routine. With 4 teenage boys, sports, household responsibilities, a career, dog and partner, I can't leave success to chance! And here I review my week ahead, ensuring proper connection and communication with the people who need to be in the know. Whether it's a car service, Dr's visit or evening work event, I plan out the week ahead. Then each night I review the plan for the following day. Knowing my brain is wired for the path of least resistance, I don't leave success to chance. That said, the unexpected happens so maintaining an ability to adapt and be flexible is critical. The balance and flex is still a work in progress for me (I'm human too!) but what I know for sure, based on science and personal experience, is that a productive, feel-good day rarely happens by accident. In the words of Benjamin Franklin, *"If you fail to plan, you are planning to fail."*

- 3 Most Important things: Each morning, consider what the 3 most important things are that need to get done. And book it in your calendar. Protect that time like you'd protect a newborn baby. I typically book the bulk of my morning as a recurring meeting to do this work because it's my best thinking time and when my energy and focus is the highest. It's not the time of day I want to spend in meetings because once the afternoon comes, I'm already on the backend of my day energy and focus wise. Consider when you are most energized and able to think clearly and problem solve. Is it possible to even once a week block that time in your calendar to do strategic work? Once you experience the impact this has on your wellbeing and output, you will begin to guard this time in your calendar, becoming a critical strategy in reaching your goals. This helps in your planning too as each Sunday night when you sit down to plan your week, you can slot in high priority thinking items that need your attention into these blocks. Extra tip: I put my 3 most important things on a stick note on my computer because I inevitably get distracted, and seeing the sticky note pulls me back to where my focus needs to be.

- Just Say "NO!": Gasp! Does the idea of saying "no" make you break out in hives? No really is a complete sentence. I'm specifically referring to it in the context of meetings. In our meeting heavy work culture, learning to discern what meetings you say YES/NO to is critical for your wellbeing and performance. If you've ever wondered where a day went, this is for you. Perhaps you regularly notice that you're busy doing 'things' all day, however you have little to show for it at the end; you find yourself wondering what you actually accomplished. One thing I know for sure is that we must control our calendar (or it will control us). Controlling your calendar is about choosing what will get your attention on any given day. Do you *really* need to attend all the meetings that have your day booked solid? Who else is going? What's the purpose and objectives of the meeting? If it's not clear why you're supposed to be there, take the responsibility of asking. Is there someone else who would be better suited to attend; someone who could go in your place who could give and extract more value? We often lose so much of our precious time on autopilot, going to meetings because we're invited, allowing ourselves to be pulled away from our most important work. Turn off autopilot and jump into the driver's seat and own your work day. When in that driver's seat, get clear on the top 3 things that MUST be completed so that you can consider your day a masterpiece (or another term that will work for you!). Your most important work is waiting! Without this kind of focus, it's far too easy to allow other people's emergencies and priorities to hijack yours.

b) ***Do*** Your Day. Stick to the plan, while also recognizing that an element of flexibility is always required. Last minute requests to edit a board report happen, as do calls from the kid's school, and other issues that require prioritization. But that's not your get-out-of-jail-free card. I see far too many "permission to interrupt" behaviors in all of us, including leaders. We interrupt in meetings both verbally and by sending private messages in the chat. We interrupt our employees with messages (expecting an almost immediate reply) when we can see from their calendar that they are in another meeting. We are also recipients of these interruptions. When interruptions constantly take you away from the work you are uniquely there to do, it's not productive. Consider how you can create a space where thinking time or desk time is protected. It's hard to accomplish much between meetings and interruptions. We teach people how to treat us, so if you are continuously dropping everything when issues come your way, others will assume that you're ok with that. Be mindful of what is distracting you from your most important work. If you have employees with a lot of last minute issues, you need daily "office hours' ' where you can take drop ins, like teacher assistants and professors at university. The main point is, we all have different realities, therefore plan and do your day based on that. Recall your job as a leader is to guide others and make decisions towards a common goal and vision. If these are your most important big rocks, are you able to say "No" to things that take your time away from your most important work? Or next time you're inclined to say 'Yes' to the next distraction, ask yourself: If I say yes to this, what am I saying no to? If the status quo isn't working for you, get curious and remain open-minded. Try something new for a few weeks and tweak it until it's a fit for you. Then keep doing it! Good habits will pay great dividends in time.

"I'm as proud of many of the things we haven't done as the things we have done. Innovation is saying no to a thousand things."

Steve Jobs

c) ***Reflect*** on Your Day. Not only does reflection help you take lessons from what went well (and what didn't), it also sets you up to use biology to your advantage! Every time we accomplish a task, no matter how big or small, our brain feeds us a reward hormone, or a dopamine kick. Our brain rewards us for these victories. This sets us up for more success and greater levels of happiness. "It can help people enjoy the daily tasks in their lives and persevere with challenges they will face by remaining optimistic about eventual outcomes." Mariana Pascha, Psychologist Some simple options are:

- What did I accomplish today that I'm proud of?
- What did I do today that moved me closer to my goal?
- What went well today?
- What do I need to do more of?
- What do I need to do less of?
- On a scale of 1-10, how effectively did I use my time today?

"When we take time to notice the things that go right - it means we're getting a lot of little rewards throughout the day."

Dr. Martin Seligman, Founder of Positive Psychology

The Myth of Multitasking

Myth: Multitasking is an effective use of time and a trick to success.

Truth: When attempting to multitask; efficiency and performance drop dramatically. In fact, productivity drops as much as 40%[18].

Focus on The Task at Hand

Think you multitask well? You might not like what the research says. Multi-tasking, as the word itself suggests, is defined as a person's ability to do more than one thing at a time. Sure, we can walk and chew gum at the same time. But try doing

[18] Steinhorst, C. (2020, February 20). *How Multitasking Erodes Productivity And Dings Your IQ.* Forbes. https://www.forbes.com/sites/curtsteinhorst/2020/02/20/how-multitasking-erodes-productivity-and-dings-your-iq/?sh=72bc8a4b3b7e

two things at the same time that require brain power. Well that's a different thing altogether. Talking on the phone and driving is a pretty well-known, much talked about, and studied example on multi-tasking that continues to get widespread attention. And rightly so! In 2020 distracted driving was the leading cause of accidents in the province of Ontario, Canada, accounting for about 64 percent of all accidents, surpassing drunk driving and speeding. We may think we can focus on two things well at once, but the data tells us otherwise.[19]

Less is More

"The (person) who chases 2 rabbits catches neither."

Confucius

It turns out that multitasking reduces our efficiency and performance because our brains can only focus on one thing at a time. And if that seems hard to swallow, get ready for this. Researchers at Stanford University found that regular multitaskers who believe they are superstar multi-taskers underperformed in all tasks in the research[20]. This even surprised the researchers. The multi-taskers appeared to be so distracted by the "noise" around them that they were constantly paying attention to all the information, unable to filter out the unnecessary pieces of information. And these multi-taskers were also slower at switching from one task to another as compared to non-multi-taskers.

According to University of Southern California (USC) Dornsife research, multitasking leads to significantly more mistakes and those who multi-task retain less information;

---

[19] (n.d.). *Distracted Driving Facts and Stats you Should Know.* ISure. https://isure.ca/inews/distracted-driving-facts-and-stats/

[20] GORLICK, A. (2009, August 24). *Media multitaskers pay mental price, Stanford study shows.* Stanford News. https://news.stanford.edu/2009/08/24/multitask-research-study-082409/

shockingly it can change the way our brain works! So next time you're in a meeting and answering emails, recognize that you will not retain much of either the email exchange or meeting content. And if that doesn't turn you off the idea of multi-tasking, research from the University of London has found that multi-tasking during thinking tasks experienced IQ scores similar to what would be expected had they smoked marijuana or stayed up all night.

How to Stop Multitasking

It's time to pull back the curtain on the myth of multitasking and return to focused time so you can take care of yourself, your team, and your results! In addition to the strategies outlined in the above Myth of Always On, there are a few additional strategies you can leverage (and encourage your team members and colleagues to do too):

1. Acknowledge that stopping multi-tasking is a personal responsibility and choice. It is not a one-time decision but requires daily commitment and diligence. We are resisting all the rings, dings and distractions that our world has come to besiege us with. Only you have the ability to effectively navigate your workday.
2. Pay attention to when you become distracted or feel disjointed. You will shift from mediocre to marvelous as you and your team accomplish what you set out to get done.
3. Turn distractions off when you're doing focused thinking work (dings, rings, and buzzes). Better yet, put your phone in another room, out of reach or earshot while you're doing your thinking work. Research has shown that having our cell phones nearby (even when not in use) is a distraction to our brain. We simply cannot resist. It's similar to a term referred to as "Shiny Object Syndrome" – getting distracted by something, before you finish what you started. Turn off your email

notifications, set your Skype or IM to "Do not disturb". Your productivity will increase! "We all understand the joys of our always-wired world—the connections, the validations, the laughs … the info. … But we are only beginning to get our minds around the costs, if we are even prepared to accept that there are costs." Andrew Sullivan

4. Remove the term and notion of "multitasking" from your vocabulary and job descriptions. Instead consider what the requirement is for the job. Perhaps it is the ability to handle multiple projects and timelines in parallel. BUT NOT SIMULTANEOUSLY! Be clearer on what it is you're looking for candidates to be able to do, but please stop with the multitasking.
5. Talk to your team about the personal boundaries you have set to establish and maintain personal and professional productivity and wellbeing; explore together how they can do the same in the context of their job role and physical environment. This becomes increasingly difficult with the popularity of open workspaces. And what works for one won't work for another. It also depends on the type of work one is doing. Consider over the course of a day the different type of work you engage in. Hammering through emails may require a different environment than working on a strategic or detailed proposal where an interruption may completely derail you.
6. Be intentional about when you switch tasks as opposed to being drawn to the next shiny object. Instead of being distracted by the rings and dings of our 24-7 connected world, when in your coveted "thinking time" turn them off, close your browsers otherwise they simply invite distraction that is not so simple to ignore.
7. Slow. Down. Take a breath. Think. Go for a walk. Close your office door and meditate for 5 minutes. While it may feel like you're getting less done, your creativity,

quality of work and overall productivity will soar. Meditation and mindfulness are like gym for the brain. Taking care of our brains in this world where we are inundated with an abundance of information whether we ask for it or not is taking its toll. Good leaders can create this space and steal moments, thus using their minds to sharpen their edge.

A word of caution: This will be difficult! In a world where we want, expect and give immediate feedback, you will need to be diligent and disciplined in finding something that works for you in the context of your work environment. What I can say is, doing what we are currently doing is not sustainable, healthy or productive. It's not helping you, your employees or your organization to flourish. I encourage you to consider this data, discuss it with your team, and see what their thoughts are. Explore what's possible. *Is there one small thing they could do differently to safeguard their time, to focus more, to achieve more?* Because when it comes right down to it, what humanized leaders are really after are great outcomes and happy people.

The Myth of Vulnerability

Myth: Leaders can't show vulnerability; it's a sign of weakness.

Truth: Vulnerability is the birthplace of human connection and trust; one cannot successfully lead others without it.

I recall a conversation I had with a senior leader several years ago. She admitted to me that she'd been having a hard time connecting with one of her VPs despite them having worked together for a couple of years. There was mutual respect and no apparent issue between them, yet they had not found that connection point; that feeling of comfort and ease with one another. The senior leader went on to share with me that she finally let her guard down, not knowing what else to do. In opening up to her VP, she admitted that she didn't have all the answers but wanted to talk about the distance between them and how it was impacting her work. This admission of struggle changed the dynamic and immediately created a positive shift in their relationship. The mere acknowledgment of this challenge – the willingness to be vulnerable, acknowledge the disconnect, and engage in a conversation to explore the issue together - created room for connection, discussion, and problem solving. She experienced that vulnerability is having the courage to be yourself. And that it's critical to building trusting relationships.

It is widely known and accepted that a core aspect of leadership is trust. While we throw that word around with ease, it is anything but easy to create and maintain. You don't simply trust someone because they ask you to or because they are in a position of authority. It's not automatic; it's earned. Think of someone you have a great level of trust with, someone in your personal life perhaps a partner or close friend. *The first day you met them, was the level of trust you had between you less or more than now? How was trust established, built, and nurtured?*

Trust in any relationship requires experience with someone and a certain level of connection. It may build quickly or over longer periods of time. You can't rush trust. It happens in its own due course. Time itself does not create trust. Perhaps there's a boss or someone in your personal life who has been around for a long time and yet a strong relationship of trust has not been built. In contrast, we can meet people and quickly, due to a situation or series of events, establish a trusting relationship. Trust gets built through shared experiences with others. This means there are endless opportunities as a leader to either build (or erode) trust with those you lead. In every interaction you have with another person, you can choose to be yourself, share openly, be vulnerable and build trust or remain guarded, private, and safe. Humanizing leadership requires the courage to be vulnerable.

There's No Leadership Without Vulnerability

"You have to be honest and authentic and not hide. I think the leader today has to demonstrate both transparency and vulnerability, and with that comes truthfulness and humility."

Howard Schultz, former CEO of Starbucks

Great leadership requires significant vulnerability. And most of us avoid it wherever possible because it takes great risk to open up to another person or group of people. Consider for a moment the vulnerability of a turtle when it sticks its head out from inside the safety of its hard shell, exposing its soft and easy-to-injure flesh. It's risky and potentially unsafe. In this way, turtles are akin to leaders. When we lead others we must go first – stick our necks out so to speak – to show others it's safe to step forward, trust us and follow where we are guiding them. For the leader who does this, like the turtle sticking its neck out from within the safety of its shell, it makes us feel exposed, leaving us open to be hurt or injured in some way – emotionally, physically or career-wise. And that's the definition of vulnerability – taking risk and opening yourself up to potential harm. It takes courage to open up to another person when you're not 100% convinced that what you have to share will be safe with them.

There's also a long-held belief that leaders need to have all the answers and if they let their guard down, they will expose their weakness or lack of knowledge which will make them appear inferior or inadequate. In actual fact, the opposite is true! The best leaders I have worked with are ones who brought together a collection of different experts in their respective fields; individuals knew ***more*** about a particular domain area than the leader. In these leaders and on the team was vulnerability, collaboration, sharing of accountability, connection, leveraging of strengths, empowerment, and the list goes on. These leaders were not threatened by vulnerability or by sharing their lesser strengths and knowledge gaps. Instead it served to strengthen their relationships, the teams they hired, and the results they produced together. This helps also to create psychological safety, a term coined by Amy Edmunson in 1999, which involves having the confidence that candor and vulnerability are welcome[21]. And being in a position of power, you have the responsibility to create it.

How to Be Open Without Oversharing

Being selectively vulnerable is hard, and it's critical to building trust with others. What I have observed in my 20+ years in leadership and Human Resources is leaders struggling with what and how much to share. There seems to be either over or under sharing, both of which can limit or damage psychological safety and/or performance. As a recovering over-sharer, I have 2 simple, helpful go-to questions I now ask myself when determining what and how much to share:

1. Will sharing this information ***help*** or ***hinder*** my team/team member in their job?
2. Will sharing this information ***strengthen*** or ***sabotage*** the trust my team/team member has in me as their leader?

With these questions in mind and also reflecting on your own experiences, can you recall times where your leaders have shared/held back in ways that were both a help and a hindrance? Have you ever been in a situation where your leader shared something that harmed your ability to do your job? Perhaps it created too much uncertainty or stress and you struggled to know what to do with the information or how to use the information productively? Or have you experienced a situation where a leader withheld information that hindered your ability to move forward successfully, to write a report, or deliver a project? Perhaps you've had a leader share confidential information with you that

[21] Hugander, P., & Edmondson, A. C. (2021, June 22). *4 Steps to Boost Psychological Safety at Your Workplace*. Harvard Business Review. https://hbr.org/2021/06/4-steps-to-boost-psychological-safety-at-your-workplace

helped you better do your job and navigate the waters. What can you learn from and take away from these experiences so you can be the leader that shares information that helps (not hinders) relationships and performance?

Increase Your Tolerance for Discomfort

It was at a 6 am spin class - a usual for me. I loved the feeling after a ride: the sense of community riding alongside others, the stress relief, and the increased focus it gave me in my workday. That's what kept me showing up week after week. This one day in particular stands out in my mind because the ride was particularly difficult. Each pedal stroke felt harder, each hill seemed higher. I felt like quitting, my confidence wavered, and I questioned the ability of my legs to carry me through the ride. I wondered why I was there instead of home in my cozy bed. Upon reflection, the only reason I kept going was because I was too embarrassed to hop off the bike and leave the ride mid-class. I didn't want others to see me quit. I did however, vow never to go to a spin class ever again.

And then my instructor Andrea shouted something I'll never forget - a phrase I've repeated time and time again - "it never gets easier, you just get stronger".

In the moment it helped carry me through the class however, its real and lasting impact happened after class when I reflected on Andrea's words. I came to realize that uncomfortable things don't become comfortable over time. It's our ***tolerance*** for being in the discomfort that grows. And that is what makes us stronger; more willing and able to dig into and do the hard things. All this time I had been thinking I was doing something wrong, needing to figure out how to decrease the discomfort of difficult situations or thorny conversations. It's HUMAN to feel uncomfortable in these situations. What a relief it was to acknowledge that. Whether a hard hill in a spin class, a challenging situation with my kids, or a difficult conversation at work, hard things don't get easier - you get stronger. It's like the more you do hard things, the stronger that grit "muscle" gets to persevere through the mud - the tough stuff. The only way past the discomfort is to feel your way through it and keep going, just like I kept going and persevered through the 8 minute hard climb in my spin class.

Leaders often have to deal with people's feelings, fear, and failures. *Comfortable?* Not usually. *Necessary?* Always. Leaders who are willing to sit in a space of discomfort with a desire to listen and communicate what needs to be said in a direct and respectful way, build trust, connection and followership. Sometimes this place of discomfort involves not knowing the answers, having the courage and confidence to say that, and communicating your belief in our ability to solve it together. Together we can do hard things.

I've known leaders who beat around the bush for fear of hurting an employee's feelings, who don't know the answer but refuse to admit it, and then others yet who tell-it-like-it-is while leaving a path of human destruction in their wake. None are helpful or productive. Often they cause harm.

We have all experienced how dynamic, uncertain, and complex our lives can become, the COVID-19 global pandemic a prime example. Schools closed, businesses laid off employees and/or sent them home to work, community centres and stores were closed, and the list goes on. Understandably citizens and employees look to their political and business leaders for certainty, clarity, and a way forward. Leadership was tested in ways I've never seen before.

We yearned for connection with others during physical distancing, and for a feeling of safety in a situation that was anything but certain or known. In the crisis, all of our basic human needs were in jeopardy. Strong leaders were needed more than ever. A leader's tolerance for discomfort and their ability to show up with vulnerability and compassion while at the same time offering a promise of hope for the future was the task. What a responsibility!

During the pandemic (and still now) I lived in Canada's capital city, Ottawa. Sophie Grégoire Trudeau, our Prime Minister's wife, contracted the COVID-19 early on in Canada's outbreak and our country's leader, Justin Trudeau, was immediately in self-isolation for 14 days. Party lines aside, I believe most Canadians would be hard pressed not to speak favourably about how our PM initially handled himself and this crisis during personal and professional uncertainty. Talk about an uncomfortable ***and*** uncertain position, a situation that threatened his loved one's safety AND the country he served as leader.

It's an example of how those who show up with humility, purpose, truth, and hope rise in times like this. New leaders emerge while leaders out of their depth will fall (eventually). In crisis we see the true character of those around us.

So how can we prepare for and strengthen our tolerance for uncertainty? It's definitely not waiting for uncertainty to strike, but instead preparing for it. Here are 4 steps to strengthen your tolerance:

1. Be self-aware. Use "1-2-3 Switch" to pause. Then observe your thoughts, feelings and actions. Notice how others are behaving. Respond accordingly with wise thought and aligned action.
2. Know your values. Live your values. While this won't eliminate discomfort, it does create clarity on what you need to say and do. It brings meaning and purpose to the discomfort. It makes it worthwhile. This is what it means to align your Will (intention), your Words (what you say), and Way (what you do). Think about a time when you've made a hard decision because it was values-aligned. Then think of a time you made a decision or took an action that wasn't aligned with your core values. For each of these situation consider these questions:

    - What was the situation?

- What happened?
- What did you do or say?
- How did it work out?
- What was the impact on you, others, and the task?
- Did you want to do or say something else?
- What did you learn?

3. Build a muscle for feeling fear and doing what needs to be done anyway. *How do you do this?* There are standalone books written on this topic and I spend many coaching hours with clients on this very topic. It starts with becoming aware of what your inner voice is saying to you. Are you aware of your inner narrator? The one that either is your biggest critic or best coach? The nagging voice can get really loud when you're doubting your abilities. I've named this voice of mine Sally. She's said things that include: "You can't do that – you're not smart enough," or "You aren't qualified for that job, don't even try!" or "You're not creative, what makes you think you can write a book?". The myth is that voice keeps us small and safe but the truth is it limits our ability to do what's brave. Becoming aware of our inner narrator is the first step to overcoming discomfort. Pay attention for a week and listen to what he or she says to you. *When does your Sally pump your tires or deflate them?* Awareness is key. Write down your insights. Then, gift yourself a few quiet moments, to take a look at your list. This second step is a challenge. *Is your thought true? Is it really true that you're not creative enough to write a book or that you're too unfit to go to the gym? What evidence do you have that makes it true?* The third step is to reframe. Ask yourself *"What else could be true? And what else?* Here you'll start to explore other options that could be equally true. The final step is to rephrase. This is where having a growth mindset is powerful. Using my real-life example of "You're not creative enough to write a book", I rephrased it to "I'm going to use my creativity

to write a book." You'll notice here that I didn't go to the opposite extreme and make a statement that is so over the top that I couldn't possibly believe it – that doesn't work. But it stretched me. It was also true. And I could believe it. I used it a lot in writing this book. I felt the fear and I wrote anyway.

4. Seek progress, not perfection. I have teenage boys and am in the throes of high school essay writing. Rewind the clock for a moment. Do you remember when you first started writing essays? It is quite the multi-step process to get from instructions assigned, to good copy being submitted. I recall the process vividly. I'd hand in an outline to the teacher, sharing my proposed thesis statement, 3 main supporting points, and examples for each of the 3 main points. I'd get feedback, revise, and write my rough draft. That draft would get reviewed by a peer or two before revising once again. Only then would the final essay be written and submitted for grading. I'm suggesting we take this approach in our leadership development, actually in all our development. I see so many examples of people showing up as beginners and expecting mastery on their first try – it's as if they're expecting they can submit their final essay without going through the other steps. Vulnerability is not easy. You'll dabble in it, perhaps dip a toe in, wade up to your ankles or retreat before you try again. That's the progress we're going for, not perfection.

"At some point, you have to stand out from behind the curtain and show people what you stand for."

Miyoko Schinner

CHAPTER SEVEN

Challenge Assumptions

> *Assumptions are like a shortcut. You have to ask yourself: Is the time you saved worth the scenery you missed?*

"The Idiot on the Highway"

This is a short story courtesy of a colleague, friend, author[22] and 10x Grammy-Award winning storyteller Valerie Gordon .

> Last evening I wrapped up a speaking engagement in NYC and was driving home on the West Side highway when a car behind me began flashing its lights in my rearview mirror.
>
> Annoying.
>
> Before I knew it, that car raced up beside me, honked, and then quickly cut in front of me, dangerously slowing and putting on his flashers.
>
> What the heck?
>
> I move into the other lane to get away from this idiot. As I pass him, he's gesticulating his hand out the window.
>
> I figure he's giving me the finger. What an ass.
>
> Then I see he's pointing. At me. And my car.

---

[22] Gordon, V. (2021). *Fire Your Narrator!: A Storyteller's Guide to Getting Out of Your Head and into Your Life.* Commander-In-She, LLC.

That's when I realize I'm driving without headlights.

I had swapped cars with my husband. His does not have automatic lights. In the bright lights of the city, I hadn't noticed. On the highway, this was soon to become dangerous.

I'm the Idiot on the Highway.

This other driver was merely trying to alert me.

I turned on my lights and waved my hand out the window in thanks. And as he passed me, he gave a thumbs up.

The moral of the story:

Things aren't always what they seem. Presume the best in people, not the worst. Always strive for communication and understanding.

And... make sure your headlights are on at night.

Why We Make Assumptions

An assumption is something we believe to be true without proof. In our daily lives we are constantly (and subconsciously) making assumptions to move through and cope in our world; to make sense of what's happening to us, by looking around us. It's an efficient way for our brain to process the world. Consider this - our brain is 2% of our total mass and yet uses 20% of our energy. Simply put, our brain saves energy when it makes assumptions, preferring shortcuts and the path of least resistance. This is both brilliant and sneaky! Brilliant because of its energy efficiency and ability to quickly process information that keeps us out of harm's way; but sneaky in that it's doing so with partial, incomplete information. It's relying on past experiences and pieces of knowledge to piece together a complete puzzle when many pieces are missing.

Human relationships are also based on assumptions too, which influence how we relate to others. Rewind back to high school math for a moment. Think of the assumptions we'd make in solving problems in math class. Unlike math class however, where we'd state our assumptions at the top of the page before working through the solution; with people and their behavior, not only don't we state them, typically we aren't aware that we're making assumptions. Our brain organizes the information we take in through the lenses of our beliefs, values, experiences, and attitudes. Can you imagine some of the issues this creates?

This highlights the importance of leaders becoming students of people - their motivators, fears, and behavior. The power of being aware of our wired tendency to make assumptions, can help us assume less, enable us to catch ourselves when we do, and act as a catalyst to challenge our assumptions. Nobel-prize winner, physicist Arno Penzias at a Fast Company Conference, said: "Change starts with the individual.So the first thing I do each morning is ask myself, 'Why do I strongly believe what I believe?' Constantly examine your own assumptions."

In their book *Unleashing the Power of Unconditional Respect: Transforming Law Enforcement and Police Training,* authors Jack Colwell and Chip Huth wrote:

We automatically tend to assume the following:

- The way I see something is the way it is.
- The way I feel about someone is the way he or she is.
- The way I remember an event is the way it was.
- If you disagree with me, you are stupid, a liar, or psychotic (disconnected from reality).

The irony is that this assumptive thought base (all problems and misunderstandings are external to me) IS the apex of self-imposed ignorance, deception, and even psychosis. Probably the only reason it is not considered pathological is that it is endemic.

So practice the pause - the space in between observation and reaction - where you can mindfully test your assumptions. With simple questions like, what does all this mean? What assumptions might I be making here? What could we do to help shift the situation? What else? What or who have we not considered? In our race to get more done and faster, we often have our blinders on, racing around a break neck speed doing "all the things." The power of the pause is a simple and underutilized tool that can significantly improve our ability to ask questions, connect with others, gain new information and insights, see situations and problems more fully, and respond with intention and thoughtful solutions that have greater impact and better results.

My "Idiot on The Highway" friend is an amazing person, not at all bad or mean-spirited. What she is is human. In our attempt to quickly make sense of a situation, our brain relies on past experiences, the beliefs we've collected from our parents, culture and life! It feels awful when we realize in an instant that we were so wrong and had totally misread a situation or person, doesn't it?

When Assumptions are Bad for Business

I have facilitated this exercise as part of Stratford Group's award winning "Leadership for Success" Program, which is both simple and effective in helping us to recognize how often we make assumptions and stories about a situation with minimal facts. Play along!

Take a look at this image of cars in a parking lot. Imagine you and a friend are approaching these cars after leaving a restaurant where you just had dinner together. What do you and your friend say to one another about the white car? The black car to the left of it? The white truck to the right?

Perhaps…

- That jerk who drives the Mercedes thinks they're a hot shot.
- They think they are better than everyone else, taking up 2 spots like that.
- They don't want their car scratched or dented so they think they can take up 2 spots.
- I bet they didn't know that someone would have the nerve to park in that tiny spot so close to them!
- That white car isn't parked between the white lines.
- I bet it's a young kid who's driving mom or dad's car.

Looking at my list or yours, which ones of these statements are true? Underline them. Which are:

- Assumptions (you believe to be true)?
- Judgements (you assign a positive or negative value)? or
- Generalization (an inference from past experience)?
- Highlight them.

For the ones that are true:

- How do you know they are true?
- What else could be true?
- Are they really a fact?
- How do you know?

Now tally up how many statements are fact vs assumption/generalization/judgment. I already know the answer. Not many. In reality, we rely on assumptions, judgements, and generalizations far more than we rely on fact in order to weave a story together. This story becomes our inner narrative and ***the*** truth, (not merely ***our*** truth). In between the few facts are many threads of assumptions, judgements and generalizations that hold the story together.

Brene Brown shared a personal story in her book *Dare to Lead,* when one day, her husband came home from work and with his head in the fridge made a comment about there being nothing to eat. She admitted that she went off on him, assuming that he meant she should have got the groceries done or dinner made. She filled in the gaps of the story with assumptions despite the fact that it was always Steve who made the dinner, not her. Assumptions that turned out to be wrong. He simply was hungry and stated it. She shared this story to illustrate how we often fill in the gaps with our own version of the truth and respond as if it were fact.

Can you relate?

The bad news? None of us are immune to hearsay and it happens all the time. The good news? When we know better, we can do better. Awareness is empowering because it gives us the opportunity to exercise choice.

The Antidote to False Assumptions - Curiosity

Spend any time with a young child and you'll be peppered with "why?" and an assortment of other questions as the child seeks to make sense of their world. In fact at age 4, it's said that we ask 300 questions per day! Questions like why is the sky blue? Why does it rain? Why do you have so many meetings at work?

Children haven't been here for very long, so they don't yet have experiences and knowledge to make assumptions and draw conclusions like we do. They are learning the fundamentals. I loved those long "adventure" walks with my eldest son, now 18 years old. We'd explore the neighbourhood after a rainfall and every worm would excite him. He'd try to "save" the worms by putting them onto the grass. He'd ask "why?" at every corner. What a wonderful way to see the world – through the eyes of a child: a beginner's mindset. *What happened to our curiosity? When did we lose the joy and passion for learning? Why did we stop being so curious and require certainty?*

Much of what we believe is the product of our imagination and our brain piecing together facts, assumptions and judgments in a sequence that makes sense to us; that fits into our mental model of the world and the systems and structures we *know* to be true. Yet, we do not have to be victims to our wiring. No matter how strongly we believe our perspective, there are always other points of view.

Getting [and staying] Curious

A powerful and worthwhile exercise is to write the version of a story you believe to be true. Underline the facts, highlight the assumptions, judgments and generalizations. Stay curious. When you catch yourself filling in the blanks with assumptions, in that moment when you notice yourself doing this, pause and instead of making a statement ask a question. Or play the story that you believe to be true back to the person you're talking to. Then ask if you're on or off the mark. They'll tell you!

"1-2-3 Switch" is a great tool to help avoid responding automatically. With a pause and the intention to understand the truth (not merely your version of the truth), you can create connection and understanding by asking questions. The goal? To expand your thinking, see others' perspectives, and seek facts so that you can uncover more of the truth and create innovative solutions. Use your curiosity and powerful questions to discover perspectives from others involved. Recognize the assumptions and fill in the gaps with facts as much as you can. What you'll find is that instead of merely seeking and solving problems, you'll be uncovering and exploring possibilities.

Assume positive intent. Most people do not get up each morning with the intent of making someone's day miserable. Most people's primary focus is upon themselves as they go about their day including: driving to work, answering emails, attending meetings, doing tasks, getting coffee, going to the gym to get a workout in before dinner, driving home, and doing personal or family things in the evening. Nowhere on a person's "to-do" list is: cut someone off on the highway, skip in front of someone at the drive through, forget to send a client an email, or hijack someone's piece of gym equipment they were waiting to use for 10 minutes. Positive intent is the best approach until you have facts and evidence that warrant a different action. Assuming positive intent does not mean blind faith. Instead, it's assuming the best in others until you have the required information to form a decision.

"Curiosity keeps leading us down new paths."

Walt Disney

CHAPTER EIGHT

Identify Blind Spots

> *Checking your blind spots reduces the danger of what's hiding there.*

When I was 16 years old and learning how to drive, my older brother Mark decided it was important not to just ***tell*** me about a driver's blind spot but to ***show*** me. I sat in the driver's seat of my dad's grey Nissan Maxima, engine off, humoring Mark as he got out of the car and gave me instructions. I loved and respected my brother so I went along with him, but truth be told, I thought he was exaggerating about the size of the car's blind spot. Looking in my rearview mirror I saw him approaching from behind and then alongside the car, only to suddenly disappear from view. He had already instructed me to call out when he disappeared, so I did. He stopped walking, I opened the car door and looked at where he was standing. I made a mental note of where he was; closed the door and once again looked in the rearview while he continued to walk. When I saw him reappear I hollered that I could see him. He stopped, I opened the car door and looked to see where he was standing. I was shocked; jaw dropping shocked. The distance that I couldn't see him in my mirror - my blind spot - was about the length of a bus. I had **NO** idea and yet it was so important to **KNOW**. Like a blind spot on a car, we humans have blind spots too. *How can we ensure we see all we need to be effective, make decisions, and avoid overlooking anything?*

This is not a chapter on decision making, but you will be empowered to think critically and see beyond your perspective. We will explore 3 commonly overlooked or misunderstood blind spots I have observed limiting a leader's ability to think critically and make decisions: bias, failure, and lack of courage. From my vantage point as an employee, leader, consultant, and HR professional, they are all pervasive and problematic and therefore present a significant opportunity for us as leaders. Let's shine a light on the unknown with open-mindedness and curiosity in recognition of the fact that staying in the dark is not the way to greater truth and understanding. I believe exploring the dark, hidden parts of ourselves with openness and curiosity can lead to greater truth and understanding. It's in that place you see things, perhaps things you've never seen before. Then you have to make a different choice. It's there you can say: "I am turning on the light. I want to see. I don't know where the switch is but if I keep feeling and exploring, I'll find what I need to know because I'll have done the necessary work to activate my vision and sight." Let's shine the light on the blind spots of bias, failure and courage, so we can elevate our leadership, decision making, and humanity.

Blindspot 1: Bias

Know Your Biases

To be biased is to be human. Just like the blind spots in our car. We don't shame or blame the car for having a blind spot. We simply know it's a thing and take action to mitigate its reality. We don't ignore the fact our car has a blind spot otherwise we risk injuring or killing ourselves or others. Human biases are like our car's blind spot - a mere fact we need to know and acknowledge, not ignore and feel shame about. When we accept and recognize our biases, we can then take corrective action. It serves no one to say: "I'm not biased". That's like driving your car and saying: "My car doesn't have a blind spot". Instead, it serves to KNOW our biases (blind spots) and take the right action otherwise we are like a horse walking around with blinders on.

There has been a lot of research and education over the last few decades on bias as it relates to Diversity & Inclusion, but I'll save bias as it relates to that topic for Chapter 9 – Foster Equity & Belonging. What I'd like to explore here are some other common biases all human beings fall prey to and how they distort our thinking and decision-making as leaders. Universal biases are very well studied in the field of psychology and also show up in textbooks for those who study HR and business. These are not judgments on you, merely a trait of what it means to be human. And knowing these is critical to your ability to understand, connect with, and lead others. It increases your competence as a leader. Increasing awareness that biases naturally exist within us helps to identify them when they surface, and prepare us with how to respond when we're faced with them. Our ability to make sound decisions based in fact while mitigating natural human biases is improved. It's another example of how important it is to become a student of people once you decide leadership is your path. Businesses may be great within their technical domain, but consistently across industries, the "people leadership" competence is lacking. Let the lessons continue!

While there are many biases that naturally exist within each of us as human beings, the two I'll elaborate on are negativity bias and confirmation bias.

1. Negativity Bias

We are predisposed to notice, react to, and remember negative images and experiences. Have you ever noticed how it's easier to recall the bad things that happened in a day than the good? It's so much easier to complain about the things that have gone wrong than notice and comment on the things that have gone well. Do you ever get caught in a loop of replaying in your mind negative things that have happened over the course of a day, or events from your life? Do you feel the sting of criticism more powerfully than the joy of praise?

The good news is that you're not alone. The bad news is our brains are wired for negativity. We have survived on this earth as long as we have because we are designed to watch for and pay more attention to the negative than the positive. Imagine it as an imbalance as to how we process good and bad occurrences in our lives. (See figure)

Printed with permission @theawkwardyeti

I went for a hike on a beautiful fall day with my family and the leaves were just turning color. We had a great time together with lots of laughter and spectacular views. On the drive home we were re-routed on a 30-minute detour because of a car accident that had closed the road back home. What stood out in our minds about the hike? The 30-minute detour. Unless we are intentional about looking for and focusing on the good (in this case the laughter, togetherness, and the views) our minds naturally gravitate to the negative (the detour in this case).

When we rewind the hands of time thousands of years back to the days where our ancestors had threats all around them, there was a greater need to pay attention to the things that could cause harm. And by "Harm", I mean death. Lions and tigers and leopards! Yes, these were the dangers for our ancestors 200,000 years ago and the reality of what they had to contend with. This meant that being more attentive to negative stimuli played a useful role in humans' survival. Hello fight-flight-freeze response. Imagine all those years ago taking a moment to enjoy the sunshine and "Smell the roses" while predators prowled and preyed upon your young. That old part of our brain, often referred to as the reptilian brain, is what kicks that fight or flight into action during threat.

While we are generally not contending with life or death situations in most of our workplaces today, it explains why under stress or overwhelm at work that we respond automatically with the fight or flight response. We interpret a threat. Heart rate increases; we may start to sweat, blood moves away from the part of the brain responsible for decision making, deliberate thought, self-control and reasoning; and to the muscles of our body in preparation for fight or flight. Despite the fact it's no longer a lion or tiger to fight or flee from, our brain and body still reacts to our stressor in the ways of our ancestors - an impulsive, reactionary and/or emotional manner.

This means many of us are living in our busy brain (where we react with emotion and on impulse) more than our thinking brain (where we respond with self-control and reason). Combining our natural tendency to notice and focus on the negative, negativity bias can further skew how we look at people and budget decisions. This impacts how we hire, promote, assess performance, give raises, provide feedback to employees, end employment (who goes, who stays), training and developing others, assigning work/tasks, decisions around corporate restructuring, etc. It highlights the importance of having to be intentional, "1-2-3 Switch", in order to maintain self-awareness. Focus on good events and positive acts in order to counterbalance the history of the negative weight.

A mindset of grounded optimism and positivity takes intention and ongoing nurturing. As fitness takes regular training, optimism and positivity, it isn't a one-and-done thing. Turn on the news and keep a tally of positive to negative news stories. Not only are we wired to pay closer attention to the negative; fear-based and negative messages bombard us. We have to be vigilant and consistently show up each day with self-awareness, curiosity and calm to notice good events and positive acts, and to seek out facts to best mitigate the impact of negativity bias. Great leadership and decision making depend on it.

To further develop your ability to see the positive and train your brain to seek out and notice the good, try this exercise at home. Dr. Martin Seligman calls this exercise simply what it is: Three-Good-Things Exercise and talks about it in his book *Flourish*[23]. While it may seem simplistic, his research has found it helps to lessen depression and increase happiness. Try it for a week and see what happens!

- Every night for the next week, set aside 10 minutes before you go to sleep.
- Write down three things that went well today and why they went well. Record in a journal or on your computer. What's important here is that there is a record.
- Beside each positive event, answer the question: *Why did this happen?*

  Seligman emphasizes that the things you write don't have to be earth shattering, although they can be. I'll share a couple of my own entries as an example: *1. I had a really fun game of driveway basketball with the boys today. We laughed a ton and enjoyed our time together. This happened because I knew today was going to be sunny and I intentionally made the time in my day to spend with them. My 4 boys are all teenagers, so these things don't happen by accident anymore! 2. Jay (my partner) and I played*

23 Seligman, M. (2013). Flourish: *A Visionary New Understanding of Happiness and Well-being* (p. 33). Atria Paperback.

indoor mini putt in our hallway. This happened because we were stuck inside during the period of COVID-19 isolation and needed a fun pick-me-up. I wanted to do something to make him smile. This did the trick.

Since doing this, I've felt lighter and noticed more good things throughout my day. It doesn't make the negative disappear, but it makes the negative less heavy or overpowering. It means while negative experiences are still there, there is a counter-balance with the positive experiences from that day. My life feels more manageable and balanced. This exercise, along with others already suggested earlier in this book including meditation, are like gym for the brain. We go to the gym to work out our body, to keep it healthy; this is your brain gym!

I've always treasured family dinners as a time to reconnect after a day apart, to laugh and to share together. I've come to make this an evening ritual at my dinner table with my boys. I am very fortunate to have grown up that way myself and I am grateful that the tradition continues with my own children. Even weekday dinners typically involve us all sitting around the table for 45 minutes to an hour. I've taken to starting our dinner table conversation with "What went well today?" What follows is sometimes funny or frivolous and then I learn why. Even with "gym class" or "recess" as the answer, responses that often have us parents rolling our eyes or sighing, I've come to learn more about my children when they share *Why*. Sometimes it's because they won the "Tournament of Champions" and I learned about their friends and how they assembled their team, but more I've been surprised by the stories of connection or kindness that they shared. It's been a gift to get a glimpse into their teenage lives and hearts. My intention is to help our boys seek the positive in their lives. The negatives are always present and obvious and I don't want to ignore them or suggest they aren't important to discuss and address - they are - but unless we are intentional about bringing the good to the surface, they rarely do. Try it! You'll be surprised at what you learn about your colleagues, team members, children and spouse.

2. Confirmation Bias

"We see the world as we are"

Anais Nin.

We see what we want to see. Perception is reality. We've all likely heard these phrases before, or something similar. Within them is a grain of truth; they are rooted in psychology. Recalling from Chapter7: Challenge Assumptions, our perception of reality is skewed because our brains look for shortcuts in order to conserve energy and to quickly make sense of our situation. Let's layer on another shortcut to become aware of – confirmation bias.

Confirmation bias refers to a cognitive shortcut where we judge people in a manner that confirms our first impression of them, or what we already believe about them. This is why "first impressions matter", because once we form an impression of someone: right or wrong, accurate or not, it's very difficult to undo that initial impression. It is also why confirmation bias is particularly problematic in leadership as it does not readily allow a person's perspective to change based on evidence. Confirmation bias can influence leaders to make non-factual assumptions and decisions, something I have witnessed many-a-time. And our workplaces are riddled with them. For example, study after study shows bias toward or against a job applicant may affect the types of questions they receive in the hiring process. This means a negative bias towards an applicant may result in the candidate being put through a very rigorous and robust set of interview questions; contrasted with a positive bias towards an applicant that results in a casual, conversational type interview. A 2018 Mercer study found that employers tend to see women as less confident than their male counterparts, which can lead to women unfairly being passed over for promotion and potentially confirming our belief that women aren't confident enough to be leaders.

I invite you to pause for a moment and reflect on what you have learned so far in *Humanizing Leadership*. What tools or techniques have you learned that could support you in challenging your own confirmation bias? Consider 1-2-3 Switch, what you learned about challenging assumptions, getting and staying curious. What else? How might you be able to leverage your team? While you can't completely prevent confirmation bias from happening, with awareness, mindfulness, and a strategy, you can quickly spot, mitigate, and minimize it.

Blindspot 2: Failure

Acknowledge Failure

We've heard many stories and sayings about failure being the path to success. But how widely is it embraced as acceptable? Time and time again I've heard leaders TALK about failure being acceptable; that they know making mistakes happen and that it's part of learning. I have yet to see an environment where people freely bring forward their mistakes without fear of some sort - fear of retribution, hearing about it in their annual performance review, or worse - fear of getting fired. Fear is a strong motivating factor and we're hardwired to avoid situations that threaten us. Is it any wonder why we avoid it?

I like the engineering design process. It builds experimentation and redesign into the planning. It's a process that ***knows*** there will be a number of tries along the way to find what works. It's not called failure nor is it looked at as failure. It's "test-evaluate-improve". This is in stark contrast to what I commonly see in organizations which have no room in schedules (or within their mental model) for failure. Instead, when failure happens, it is something that's hidden due to fear, or stressful to fess up to. If you're lucky, it won't show up in your performance review. *Why is there any wonder employees are risk and failure averse?* There's no psychological safety here.

How can you shift the feeling and culture around failure within your own team? So that there's no shame in creating, trying, and improving; that finding results different from your original expectations are embraced and not considered something you need to apologize for and fix? How can one interpret and embody failure in a positive, productive way versus a negative and non-productive way? How can you show vulnerability about your own failures to model the way? As a leader you must go first!

Growth Mindset

Carol Dweck, American psychologist and Professor of Psychology at Stanford University known for her work on the psychology of mindset believes it starts with what she has termed a "growth mindset" and contrasts it with the opposite – a "fixed mindset". Essentially it boils down to the idea that we can't grow, learn, create and innovate without, what we label as, "failures" along the way; we can't master a domain or skill without them. Success is born from repeated failures and trying again. Dweck summarized her work in a Harvard Business Review[24] article succinctly: *"Individuals who believe their talents can be developed (through hard work, good strategies, and input from others) have a growth mindset. They tend to achieve more than those with a more fixed mindset (those who believe their talents are innate gifts). This is because they worry less about looking smart and they put more energy into learning. When entire companies embrace a growth mindset, their employees report feeling far more empowered and committed; they also receive far greater organizational support for collaboration and innovation. In contrast, people at primarily fixed-mindset companies report more of only one thing: cheating and deception among employees, presumably to gain an advantage in the talent race."*

When I first read Dweck's book I had three pre-school aged boys and was working part-time in the learning and development

---

[24] Dweck, C. (2016, January 13). What Having a "Growth Mindset" Actually Means. *Harvard Business Review.* https://hbr.org/2016/01/what-having-a-growth-mindset-actually-means

field. It was important to me that I both contributed to my career in a meaningful way and be the mother I wanted to be. Since my early 20s I've been an avid reader and over the last 20ish years mainly on the topics of: motivation, positive psychology, spirituality and leadership. I came across Dweck's book *Mindset: The New Psychology of Success: How We Can Learn to Fulfill our Potential* and it profoundly impacted my perspective and language around effort, failure, and success. It influenced my own mindset, words and actions. I immediately shifted the way I parented, coached others, and facilitated workshops. The example of failure that comes to mind, that I used with my boys for years, until it didn't seem they needed the external reminder any longer, was "Don't say I can't – try again or ask for help." Simple but not easy until it became their automatic "go to" response when they were faced with setbacks. Not all three boys embraced it with the same vigor. However, there was one son whose natural tenacity, grit, and fire in the belly resonated well with this message. He now had the words to convey what he really wanted and needed in order to gain mastery over whatever he wanted to focus on. He was a determined little soul and with this tool flourished. The other two embraced the "not yet" perspective with different levels of enthusiasm. Now, all of them are in their teens and they have integrated Dweck's growth mindset. What a difference the way they talk to themselves about effort and failure has made in their school, friendships, sports – in all parts of their lives. This lays the foundation to becoming a humanized leader and it's never too late to adopt it.

One of the things I noticed that helped with the integration of a growth mindset in our home was the willingness to be open in sharing the feelings associated with our setbacks. It was ok (and encouraged!) to talk about the disappointment, frustration, and unmet expectations so that we could pivot, redirect, refocus, and then try again. What I have observed in my 20 years in HR is that we're missing the permission to feel (as well as fail!) and yet it's a fundamental human experience. Omitting this, treating feelings like an F-word to be avoided is a missed opportunity to learn, grow and innovate.

What I have learned is that despite what leaders are telling us, our experiences are that failure is not acceptable. That is unrealistic, unfair, and definitely doesn't set us up for innovation, high performance and personal wellbeing. It's ridiculous really. And yet it continues. Failure is accepted as a concept until it happens in reality. Imagine if we had those expectations of our young children as they were learning to walk, read, or ride a bike. We are naturally curious, inquisitive and willing to try new things; until there's an intervention of say an adult instilling fear with an "Oh be careful", or creating other barriers and restrictions that limit our willingness to try. We praise our kids on achievement not effort. We give money for grades achieved, and often don't reward the process. Failure no longer feels natural or safe despite the fact it's through failing and learning forward that we made it to this point in our lives. I hope you can start to see the opportunity that exists for you to create the space and energy for failure. The positive impact it could have on those you lead and the results you achieve. It's a total change in our thinking, mindset, and approach to leading people and projects.

Recalling the 5 Drivers that Simplify Leadership, we all have an innate need to feel safe, belong, do work that matters, and grow/learn. It's no wonder employees don't feel safe to fail because in most of our environments it's **not** safe to fail! We don't plan for failure. We say we want dissenting voices, different perspectives, opposing opinions, but this takes time to table and work through and it takes people with courage, character, competence, and compassion to lead it. We don't build this into our schedules. And if an employee is able to muster up the courage (which we'll talk more about in a few pages), they risk being rejected which rubs up against their innate drive to feel safe and belong. Failure doesn't feel safe. If you've ever wondered why your employees don't really give you the goods with what's going on, or you feel like they are holding back, this could be why. It's not enough to say. You need to show.

I want you to think of a failure you experienced - work or personal. Bring back your memory of the event: where you were, who you were with, and the details of what happened. *What was the situation? Who were you with? What were you doing or saying? What were others doing or saying? Take yourself back fully into that moment. Do you have a picture in your mind's eye?* You may need to take a moment to pause, close your eyes and really sink into it. Once you're there, *how do you feel?* I don't know about you, but there are few emotions worse than feeling like a failure. We avoid it like the plague. And yet that's what we're asking your employees to feel comfortable with and with no confidence that if they do fail, they will be accepted or that there will be a safety net there to catch them.

Can you see how failure is so inextricably connected to the earlier Practices? Environments that have not been built with acceptance of failure can bring about feelings of shame or unworthiness when failure happens. You can also see how instrumental power skills (aka soft skills) are needed in our leaders of today. As humanized leaders bravely lead us into uncharted territory, failure is bound to happen. The sooner we accept it, expect it, and plan the bounce back, the better! *"Sometimes when you innovate, you make mistakes. It is best to admit them quickly and get on with improving your other innovations."* Steve Jobs.

Make it Safe to Fail

Now you know better, how do you do better? If your opportunity is to create an environment where it's safe to make and admit (even welcome) failure, how do you make it safe to fail?

1. Accept it - We often take our lead from our own leaders. We look at what they do and from that modeling make assumptions and observations about behaviours and language that are/are not acceptable. What example are you setting for failure being ok? Do you expose your shortcomings, knowledge gaps, and mistakes? You know the old saying "actions speak louder than words" and

"lead by example". This one can start with you - accept your own mistakes. Fail first, learn from it, and share it. Expose yourself to your team and show how you recover. Be an example of what it looks like to fail, fall, and rise. This requires integrity and vulnerability and a whole lot of courage (coming up next). Is it risky? Of course. You can't be vulnerable without an element of risk. But growth and innovation don't happen in the comfort zone. One of my Peloton bike instructors reminds me "if it doesn't challenge you it doesn't change you". Make peace with imperfection. Bring back the beginner's mindset you had when you were young and trying new things; learning new concepts. Experiment, play, have fun, practice, learn, collaborate, innovate. This really is a form of art, and *where is **art** found?* In he***art***. Then you use your brain to determine the next right step, to plan and execute accordingly. Our brains are our biggest asset and can also be our greatest liability. *"You can make mistakes, but you're not a failure until you start blaming others for those mistakes."* John Wooden, successful college basketball coach.

2. Expect it – As Einstein said, "success is failure in progress". If you believe that to be true, and understand how it ends up creating better outcomes, projects, and products, expect failure in others. And let others know this! Plan for it. Talk about team failures for the purpose of learning. Make it a team norm, even a meeting agenda item. Don't criticize or punish for failures and mistakes, instead be that soft place to land when failure happens; to ensure the failure results in learnings that take you forward as opposed to mistakes that hold you back. If you want creativity and innovation, it comes with failure. Failure is the price of admission for creativity, learning and innovation and we know that there's no room for this while under stress and feeling fear. In team meetings ask about setbacks, things that didn't go as planned, and learnings for the week. Build it into your schedules and label it. Let it be known that there's space set aside to share, learn and grow together. You'll have to

be diligent in helping your organization reframe what it means to fail on your team; from a mindset of failures = I am a failure; to one of failure = I am learning. Don't expect them to follow right away because you say so. Expect them to follow your lead when you do it.

3. Bounce Back - When failure happens, what are you going to do? How are you going to react? It turns out that if we wait until the moment failure happens to figure it out, we don't do so well. In Dr. Brene Brown's research, she was surprised to find that it's safer to do the risky thing (fail), when you know how you'll bounce back and recover. You can create an element of psychological safety because you have a plan to escape the discomfort of failure when it happens. Knowing how we'll overcome our mistakes is critical to helping us fail in the first place.

How Failure can Galvanize Us

A number of years ago, on a cold and snowy winter day, my boys were at a local outdoor skating rink, just a short walk from our home. At the time, my son Cameron was still learning how to skate so he fell down a lot. One day he fell down, looked up at me and said "It's ok mummy. I can try again or ask for help." And with that he stood back up and tried again. You see, when you adopt this thinking and it becomes part of your mental model, failure is not the end; it is merely part of the process.

1. Be aware: You fail or make a mistake. Then what happens? You feel something (there's that F-word again). Awareness can speak to us through feelings in our physical bodies. Yet we don't teach people how to handle their emotions, other than to teach how to suppress them. By this point in *Humanizing Leadership*, hopefully you've examined some of your unexplored emotions, perhaps have taken an emotional intelligence assessment or watched a Daniel Goleman video on the subject. The challenge? When emotion knocks at your door, answer it. When we mess up,

we get that awful gut feeling and our survival instincts kick in to fight, flee, or freeze. All you need to do here is notice; notice the emotion at your door. That's all. Don't invite it in. Just notice it there; see it; acknowledge it; accept that it's shown up. "1-2-3 Switch" will help you to shift from reactive brain to thinking brain and clarify what to do with the emotion at the door.

2. Get curious: Remember in Chapter 7 we talked about assumptions and our uncanny knack for making up stories; to connect what few facts we have about a situation in order to make sense of our world? That's what happens here. We start making assumptions, judgments, and generalizations where facts evade us. Time to get curious. Curiosity is the antidote to assumptions and judgment. Asking questions to find out what happened, what went wrong, and/or what was missing from the plan that caused the mistake or failure not only arms us with more data, it also buys us some time to get into thoughtful and mindful presence where we can respond with greater intention that builds connection (vs. reacting automatically in a way that erodes connection with others.)

3. Try again! Embrace a growth mindset and model it for others. Dr. Dweck talks about the impact of a growth mindset and brain differences - that those with a "not yet" attitude towards making a mistake, show their brains activated in a way that indicates they are engaging with the learning and using it to push forward. In contrast,

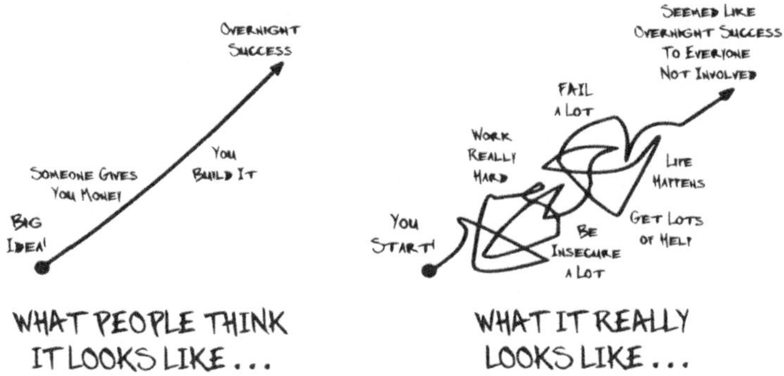

individuals with a more fixed mindset withdraw, pull back and their brains aren't activated by the failure. It actually causes poorer performance and less engagement to avoid the feeling of failure in the future. What incredible insights for leaders! You can see the importance of embodying and fostering a growth mindset in self and team. In Industry 4.0 where changing technologies, skills, and jobs are our reality, it's leaders with this mindset who will rise.

"I have not failed. I've just found 10,000 ways that won't work."

Thomas A. Edison

Blindspot 3: Courage

Build Your Courage

The root of the word courage is cor, the latin word for heart. While over time this word has become associated with bold acts of heroism, in its earliest form, courage meant "to speak one's mind by telling one's heart". If we are going to get anywhere fast in these times we need to slow down and simplify, to get back to our roots and our own foundations. This is your values and vision. With those alive and well within you, you're primed to be able to act in accordance with them. Courage is values in action.

What I know for sure is we need more courage in our businesses, community, and world leaders today. Young leaders like Malala Yousafzai[25] (activist for female education and the youngest Nobel Prize laureate and Greta Thunberg[26] (climate activist), stand up for what is right, true and just. Experienced professionals who have a lot at stake and do what's right anyway, like Cynthia Cooper who uncovered massive fraud in the WorldCom accounting books, which added up to $9 billion

[25] [n.d.]. *Malala's Story*. Malala Fund. https://malala.org/malalas-story?sc=header

[26] [n.d.]. *Fridays for Future*. Fridays for Future. https://fridaysforfuture.org/

and the imprisonment of five executives[27] and Sherron Watkins, the Enron whistleblower[28]. And like Julia Wagg[29], my forever-36-year-old-mentor who was known as a force of nature within both the business and LGBTQ+ communities. It's clear that when one charters into unknown territory, it requires a great deal of courage.

> *"It's important to be able to dig down and find your courage, which isn't always so easy. My mother would say, don't ever allow yourself to be intimidated. That was really ingrained in me, and I think that helped."*
>
> Cynthia Cooper

Years ago, I was in a team meeting along with ten of my colleagues. Our VP asked for everyone's opinion on a contentious topic. Knowing I was quite passionate and vocal, I was asked to share first. I was very intentional in my approach, wanting to be clear and kind. I knew that several co-workers in the room were of the same thought - they had told me so in private - but I was interested in hearing from others. This was the time to express and listen to different viewpoints; in the safety of our team and the four walls of the boardroom. I had the opportunity to voice my opinion and as a team member felt a responsibility of being part of the solution. I'm a firm believer that if you choose not to voice your thoughts and perspectives when asked, you lose the right to complain about it when you don't like what follows. It is up to the leader to create the space and environment where it's safe to share, challenge and together move forward.

---

27 Ripley, A. (2008, February 4). Q&A: Whistle-Blower Cynthia Cooper. *Time.* https://content.time.com/time/arts/article/0,8599,1709695,00.html

28 (n.d.). *Sherron Watkins*. National Whistleblower Center. https://www.whistleblowers.org/whistleblowers/sherron-watkins/

29 Pearson, M. (2017, April 20). Julia Wagg, 1980-2017: A force of nature in Ottawa's LGBTQ community. *The Ottawa Citizen.* https://ottawacitizen.com/news/local-news/julia-wagg-1980-2017-a-force-of-nature-in-ottawas-lgbtq-community

I took a breath and spoke my mind. It shouldn't be that bad, I thought. I knew many of my colleagues around the table felt the same. How shocked and disappointed I was when no one else spoke up; even when my VP asked for others to share their viewpoints, similar or otherwise. Silence. Never before had I experienced such a thing (although I have since).

Not only did we proceed in a way that was opposite to what the majority of us knew to be right, but I was hung out to dry. While that was not the intent of my colleagues, they lacked the courage or feeling of safety to speak up. But there was a cost. I became unfavourably known as the only (and lonely) one who would voice opposing or alternative viewpoints. Not long after, when I was seeking advice from a colleague on how to gain more traction on a project I was leading, her advice was "Look around at the people who are successful here - be like them." And in those words, right there, I knew I didn't belong. What I saw around me were smart, kind, scared, and yet silent professionals. People who were not willing or able to step up, speak out, and be heard. They had good hearts, positive intent, but their words and their actions spoke otherwise. That was not and never has been me. It was a pivotal moment in my career and it came with a huge sense of relief. I finally understood the inner struggle I'd been feeling. I grew a little that day, and for that I'm thankful.

Leaders need to be that voice, to create spaces for other voices, and to make bold and sometimes unpopular decisions. This all requires courage. Leaders need to allow and foster a safe environment for failure. And this too requires courage because it takes risk and vulnerability. These are the human skills and the power skills, in action. These are in part what make a strong leader with team members who follow because of belief, trust, commitment and curiosity. Being a leader who provides feedback and challenges ideas – this too requires courage. When you commit to humanized leadership, it doesn't ever become easy, but it certainly becomes clear.

"A real leader uses every issue, no matter how serious and sensitive, to ensure that at the end of the debate we should emerge stronger and more united than ever before."

Nelson Mandela

Do you have an example of someone in your life - personal or professional - who shows great courage? What about moments in your life where you wish a person with authority or in power had shown greater courage? It's in these small moments we have the opportunity to show courage, often have only a split-second to decide – do you lean into the discomfort and say or do what's right? Do you align your words and way with your will? Or do you ponder what to do, stay stuck in the discomfort of the conversation, remaining silent until the moment passes?

I have often wondered how the outcome could have been different for Nortel Networks, had their leaders been more courageous in this way - if their outcome could have been different. Of course, we'll never know.

What is courage exactly? Let me start by saying what it's not. It's NOT about being fearless. It is not always loud or obvious, like running into a burning house to save a life. It does not have to involve life or death decisions.

Instead courage can be found in the smallest of moments that add up over time. It's about feeling the fear and doing or saying it anyway because it's right and just. It doesn't always feel safe. If it did, I suppose it wouldn't be courage!

Courage can be found in simple moments, like speaking up in a meeting when you notice someone is constantly being interrupted. "Excuse me. [Name] was interrupted again and I'm really interested in hearing what else they have to say." It unfolds one situation at a time, and it's never easy or comfortable because it always requires some level of personal risk. Courage is a choice to stay aligned with your true north - your values and vision of who you want to be as a leader, and your commitment to showing up with integrity and compassion. When you connect with and align your will, words, and way you will always know what the next right action is. Simply pause, "1-2-3 Switch" and lean into your values and vision of who you are growing into. Your will is there; now you need to choose courage to align your words and your actions. You will always be led to what's right, even though the outcome may not be what you desire. If there's a secret to courage, that is it.

In her book *Radical Candor: Be a Kickass Boss Without Losing Your Humanity,* Kim Scott shared a simple and powerful model of communication that integrates caring personally and challenging directly. As I read through Scott's book and how she developed the model via her experience at Apple and Google, what struck me was that brave and bold leaders aren't necessarily more comfortable calling out elephants in the room. Instead they are leaders who are ***more willing*** to call out the elephants in the room, by being kind and direct. They are grounded in their values, feel the discomfort, and choose to do/say what's right. In a team where there's connection and high trust, these types of conversations may be hard, but they are embraced. The topics are not avoided but encouraged. There's no growth in comfort, so if you're waiting for comfort, you'll be waiting forever. Instead, don't wait until you're comfortable to stand up for what's right, to show up as the leader others need, or to be seen as the leader who will challenge old and ineffective organizational norms and structures. That day will never come. Feel the fear and do it anyway.

As I mentioned at the outset of this book, my goal is to equip you with the foundational principles, knowledge, and tools to level up your leadership and to inspire you to put them to use. These tools become part of your human toolbox, not merely your leadership toolbox; tools that become integrated with who you are, making you a better person in all your spaces and places. As you walk through your daily life - at work and play - you can do so with greater awareness and integrity and be that ray of hope that others are seeking. You can be that beacon of light simply by being who you are in all the spaces you occupy; and all the hats you wear.

CHAPTER NINE

Foster Equity & Belonging

> *It is not our differences that divide us. It is our inability to recognize, accept, and celebrate those differences.*
>
> — Audre Lorde

This is not going to be your typical chapter or rhetoric on diversity and inclusion. You won't read about creating policy, strategy, or be given a series of steps to implement. There are many well-written books and pieces written on these topics by people far more qualified than I. Instead, in this chapter walk with me as I pull back the curtain and give a voice, from my perspective and experience, to what I've observed being silenced in this space. I view this chapter more like a dinner table conversation, one that may get uncomfortable at times, and will be imperfect and flawed. Because I don't see how any leadership conversation is complete without it - the rawness and the flaws.

I have long held the belief that Diversity, Equity, Inclusion & Belonging (DEIB) is a topic that belongs in every single leadership book and training course. It's foundational to leadership, and yet I continue to see it as a glaring omission; a topic that is "accessory" as opposed to foundational and essential to leadership. Yet effective leadership in our world today can't exist without it. As we embark on this chapter, bring with you the learnings from prior chapters - your compassion, character, courage, and curiosity. You'll need them all because I believe in many ways we are at the most critical leadership junction of our time. Without becoming aware of, and then intentionally dismantling the barriers of discrimination and intolerance, we cannot inclusively lead others. Period. Instead we will merely perpetuate the outdated approach to leadership which has run its course – one that worked for a system and particular group of people from specific backgrounds. This no longer serves the modern world, as we strive for greater humanity and equity in our workplaces, and focus on the triple bottom line (i.e. people, profit, and planet) as a marker of success. I like the way Avinash Chandra, founder and CEO of BrandLoom puts it: *"...it can be defined as meeting the needs of the present without compromising the ability of future generations to meet their own needs.*[30]*"*

We need not look far for an example of why this topic is of critical importance in our leadership today. Movements like #MeToo and #BlackLivesMatter, among many others that have come before, are responses to inequality that persist in our society. Humanizing Leadership helps to explore and support the mindset required for dismantling and rebuilding our thinking by building a strong leadership foundation; one founded on values, emotional intelligence, and mindfulness.

As we begin this chapter that will invite reflection, learning, and new ways of thinking for those of us in a position of privilege, I'd like to introduce you to a Lego metaphor. Like many children, my boys loved Lego when they were young; building and creating for days. They would get a new Lego set, build it per the instructions, smash it up, then put the pieces into the larger Lego box with all the other pieces they had collected over time. Later, going to the big box of mixed pieces from a range of Lego sets, their creations were even bigger, better, and more fabulous than before. They chose which pieces to keep from old structures, left what pieces didn't work in the box, and discovered new pieces they wanted to add. Similarly, we can do the same with patterns

---

[30] Fernandes, P. (2023, February 28). *What Is the Triple Bottom Line?* Business.com. https://www.business.com/articles/triple-bottom-line-defined/

of thinking. Like Lego, we can break down our thinking, learn something new, drop old thinking patterns that no longer serve, and ultimately choose which pieces we move forward with to build back better. In doing so, we need to grant ourselves the space to observe our own thinking, judgments and beliefs, and then rebuild, asking ourselves: which pieces do I keep, which new pieces do I want to add, and what pieces don't serve me/our time anymore? With that permission to pick up, learn, experiment, put down or keep new ways of thinking, let us begin.

Issues of racism, gender inequity, LGBTQ+ discrimination, under-employment for persons with disabilities, ageism, and inequality in general, are not new. What is new perhaps, is how in the case of George Floyd's murder, we saw people from all walks of life come together in protest saying "enough is enough"'. Hand in hand, side by side, we saw communities stand up and speak out. It is beyond time, my friends. Let's do better. Let's be better. Each one of us in a position of power and/or privilege has a responsibility to do so. ***Yes*** our systems need a complete overhaul, ***and*** you and I right now can also start the change. Change can and does start with you and me. So ***yes*** to policy change, strategy and work plans (they are critical for scalable, sustainable change), and ***yes to*** personal responsibility and education too. It's the latter where I do my work; where I see a small window of opportunity to help. And where I see yours as a leader to make an immediate and lasting impact in the lives of those you touch every day.

A Few Definitions

I said this wouldn't be your standard rhetoric on DEIB however, here are a few terms and the definitions that I'll be using in this chapter (although I acknowledge that language is quickly evolving in this space).

Equity – I look at equity as equal access to power and equal access to participate without retribution. This differs from the Oxford dictionary definition which defines equity as a situation in which everyone is treated equally. It's a significant yet subtle difference. Let me give you an example from my life (which highlights my own privilege within the challenge). One of my boys has severe dyslexia, which was formally diagnosed when he was in Grade 2 (the challenge). At that time he wasn't able to decipher the alphabet, never mind read. As his mama, I was faced with a choice. Do I treat him and his brothers the SAME and keep him in the publicly funded school system where he doesn't have equal access to the curriculum based on his learning difference? Or at a cost, do I stream him into the private school system (the privilege) and enroll him in a school that specializes in teaching children with learning differences like his, thus providing him equal access to the curriculum as his brothers had? Unequal treatment of my boys but equal access to learning. I chose the private school route and after spending 6 years there he has not only learned to read, he has learned the value of differences, of kindness, of compassion, and of appreciating every individual for their uniqueness and strengths. He got schooling in the curriculum and, perhaps even more importantly, was schooled in inclusion, equity, and belonging.

Diversity and Inclusion – the best and simplest description I've heard for these terms was by Andres Tapia: Diversity is the mix. Inclusion is making the mix work. Another analogy: diversity is akin to being at the dance; inclusion is being asked to dance.

Belonging – this is a newer term being used in the Diversity, Equity, and Inclusion space, an example of how this language continues to evolve. And yet, when we refer back to the 5 Human Drivers that Simplify Leadership in Chapter 4, needing to belong - to be and feel a member of - has long been accepted as a requirement for humans to survive. It is a basic need we are wired to want and seek out. Loneliness, social isolation, and/or poor social relationships are associated with a myriad of health conditions. We all need to belong to live well.

In *Humanizing Leadership*, we recognize and accept that the path to inclusion for all – our north star – will take time, change, challenging the status quo, curiosity, courage, discomfort, commitment, and resources. This desire to create workplaces where everyone feels they belong is a priority within Humanizing Leadership, in fact there is no true leadership without it. And this commitment to inclusion and belonging is a call for courage because oftentimes it requires us to speak up and step up against the grain; to be the one out front, open and exposed, to make and take a stance. Being the first to do anything can be scary and uncertain. We can't be guaranteed a positive outcome, so it rocks our very instinctive need to be and stay "safe". I imagine most of us believe that in situations of injustice we'd have the courage to speak up. The truth is, most of us don't. Our brains register rejection of any form the same way as physical pain! And we subconsciously know that being ostracized from the group in which we belong threatens our wellbeing. Cleverly, our default mode has literally been wired to avoid rejection. So in situations that require one to "put their neck out" and speak up against the majority, it's quite literally painful. When we know better we can do better, so let's be part of the solution. Feel the fear and the pain and do it anyway. Lean into your values and your vision of who you are/want to be as a leader. Allow those to anchor you while you push up against the edge of discomfort with the knowledge and belief that there are times where we must do the right thing simply because it's the right thing to do. Even when it's hard. Actually, especially when it's hard.

We Must Do Better

I have cared about the uniqueness and acceptance of all people long before DEIB became a thing; before they became trendy buzzwords and organizational requirements. Growing up, my mum taught me many lessons; one of them was that kindness was the most underrated quality in another human being. As I grew, I looked at the world and my experiences through this lens and have been both stunned and saddened at how such a simple and important quality appears to be so rare. I've learned how very right she was.

In North America, workplaces have been talking about DEIB (it's had different names along the way) for well over 50 years and I have to be frank - the statistics are dismal. Gender diversity education emerged in the 1970s and 1980s, evolving into broader diversity education in the US in the 1990s and yet its efficacy has been questioned. While implicit bias training (training designed to expose people to their unconscious biases) has helped to change individual-level beliefs and actions, meta-analyses suggest it is largely ineffective in diminishing institutional inequities. In other words, it hasn't worked. I'm not saying this to lay blame or induce shame. I'm saying this to be perfectly clear that we need to do better.

Why? The data is in. Businesses do better with high-functioning diverse and inclusive teams. We've been talking about the business case for DEIB for years. I'm not going to do that here because that's been clearly established. What about the human case? Thankfully in recent years there has been more pressure on businesses to revive their moral and social conscience.

I recall a time when I was on a hiring panel for a very senior role. By far, the candidate who came out on top was a Muslim woman. The hiring manager was dubious about hiring her, which baffled me. It was clear she was the front-runner. The other candidates, who all were white males, didn't even come close. Her education and experience, knowledge, education, communication skills, her grit and passion for her profession – second to none. Finally, after much conversation about what the hiring manager meant when he argued she wouldn't "fit in", they lowered their head and admitted that they didn't think the team would accept a woman wearing a hijab in this high-level position. There we have it. This is an example of how it happens; how good people fall into the trap of perpetuating 'what is' instead of having the courage to step into discomfort and stand up for what's right. Good people making bad choices.

If you're in a position right now to influence the system through policy and programs, please do so. Read this chapter. Share it with your colleagues. Be brave. Invite others into the conversation. Take action. If your scope of influence is within your own team, start there. Take a look at your team- how diverse are they? I encourage you to consider diversity in a really broad sense – gender, culture, ethnicity, country of origin, experience, age, etc. Diversity is only part one, and typically the easiest "box" to check. But let's be clear – the value is not yet realized by simply having "the mix". Don't allow yourself to get too smug! What's been learned in the years of DEIB work is that diversity without inclusion is worse for business than maintaining a homogeneous team. Diversity without inclusion is exclusion. (Spoiler alert: individuals who have been marginalized have been telling us variations of this for years.) Inclusion takes intention, awareness, effort, education, discomfort, open communication and work. And it is oh so necessary to create workplaces that are enriching, innovative, creative, and at their heart - human. There must be psychological safety (i.e. the shared belief it's safe to share without retribution) and trust within the team where diverse voices and experiences are invited, can be expressed, accepted, and leveraged else the potential within diversity has been lost. Let's see inclusion used as a verb – an action word.

You can be the beacon of hope, optimism, and inclusion for those within your sphere of influence. You may be shocked at how large that sphere ends up being. Be open to the idea that with a genuine will to do better, the intention to show up with curiosity and courage, and in following through with the right action, it's possible to make a difference; one conversation and one person at a time. Words and commitment matter, but action matters more.

Have you noticed how many businesses almost sermonize DEIB but it's not reflected in reality? Companies making bold statements to their shareholders, employees, and customers? Putting it to print in their annual reports. Companies hanging fancy award-winning plaques with their values on their boardroom walls and website pages? And yet there's a disconnect with what many of our organizations and leaders profess with what our employees feel or experience.

If there are no losers in this quest for DEIB, what's stopping us? Like any complex and long-standing challenge there are many layers to reveal, deconstruct, and understand. I don't claim to have all the answers - I'm a privileged, middle class, Christian, cis-white woman - so I couldn't possibly. ***And*** I'm a woman who wants to use the power and privilege I do have to help bring a voice to this work with the goal of diversifying and equalizing the spaces and places where important business and governmental decisions are made. I'm committed to collaborating in community with others, to being curious together, and to co-creating a better future in our workplaces and our world; a world with a bright future that I want for my children and your children to live in. I've struggled with writing this chapter in my book. I've wrestled with who am I to write about DEIB? And I've come to the conclusion that I'm someone with a heart, a voice, and the commitment to be part of the positive change. Do I have fear of mis-speaking or offending? Absolutely. And when I hear feedback from readers about where I can do better, I will. I'll change my words and I'll align my actions. But fear can't stop me. It can't stop you. There's too much at risk to stay silent.

"If you are neutral in situations of injustice, you have chosen the side of the oppressor. If an elephant has its foot on the tail of a mouse and you say that you are neutral, the mouse will not appreciate your neutrality."

Desmond Tutu

Many leaders I work with unknowingly lead from a place of fear. Fear of being criticized. Fear of failing, or saying the wrong thing. Fear of standing out. Fear of not getting the next raise or bonus. Even fear of being fired. And so it's easier to stay safe and silent. We've already talked about how fear limits our ability to think big, make aligned choices, and connect with others. In fear, instead of being able to thoughtfully respond, we automatically react. In fear, we aren't able to challenge old systems, paradigms or thought patterns and biases. In fear, it's human nature to use our assumptions and old thinking models that have worked for us in the past to stay safe. While this is true, I also know that you want to do better. With this new knowledge, you are now able to take the right action to mitigate this aspect of human nature in contexts where it's harmful (like the boardroom).

In my experience, no other topic right now causes more fear in leaders than that of diversity, inclusion, equity and belonging. So much so that it's avoided. Not because leaders don't want a better, fairer, equitable future, but because they lack the awareness, skills, courage, or ______ (you fill in the blank) to navigate this new work reality. However, like a flashing warning light on the dash of a car, it can only be ignored for so long before something breaks. This is where your 4C's come into play so that with **c**haracter, **c**ourage, **c**uriosity and **c**ompassion you can take the next right step, then the next one, and so on.

The Changing Conversation

Changing the conversation is challenging. It's hard because we're talking about changing a conversation that is grounded in bias, many hidden and unconscious. Recall Chapters 7 (Challenge Assumptions) and Chapter 8 (Identify Blind Spots). Biases and assumptions are deeply ingrained not only in our DNA but also in our cultures, beliefs, and our systems – family, work, religion, and government. They are multi-layered and oh so complex.

When you look around the office, your kitchen table, and community gathering spots where people are doing ok; that "as things are" is working just fine, we don't often see the people on the fringes of society. The people who are excluded simply due to differences. *Who are we not welcoming in due to our underlying assumptions, biases and structures? Whose voices are not being heard?* This is not intended to elicit feelings of shame or guilt because those don't serve you or anyone else. Shame and guilt don't allow for change and growth because they keep us small and silent. It centres us in the conversation instead of focusing on the marginalized and oppressed. However, to revive the heartbeat in our organizations and communities, to bring humanity back to our interactions and teams, to thrive in a global economy, and to truly connect as human beings, we need all voices to be seen, valued, and heard.

I'd like you to think back to when you were in elementary school and there was a new child who joined the class mid-year. What happened? The new student was likely shy, anxious and/or intimidated. They were an "outsider". If you were in a school such as mine, your teacher buddied them up with another child in the class who would be kind and support their integration into the class. This child was chosen by the teacher with the belief the new friend would mentor and advocate for them; be a voice for them, support them, and help them feel like they belong. In Chapter 4 (Discover the Drivers of Motivation) we talked about our innate, human need to belong. We are social and cooperative beings by nature. Alone we do not survive. While we are now adults, we are actually no different from children in this regard - it's human nature at play. So be that child who was entrusted to help the new kid in class. Extend your hand, use your voice, and stand up for what is right. Remember your values and act in accordance with them. With those as your guide, you will never go wrong. This is courage!

Intersectionality

More recently, the term *intersectionality* has been used in the DEIB space. It reveals the layered complexity of diversity, inclusion, equity, and belonging. (See the figure below: Facets of Intersectionality). The Oxford dictionary defines intersectionality as *the interconnected nature of social categorizations such as race, class, and gender as they apply to a given individual or group, regarded as creating overlapping and interdependent systems of discrimination or disadvantage*. I believe unpacking this term and concept is a critical starting point in order for greater understanding, compassion, and ultimately equity in our workplaces.

I look at intersectionality as all the parts that make us who we are. Some of those "parts" may include elements of our identities that are disadvantaged or marginalized in our society. The more disadvantaged elements we identify with, the harder it is to be seen, valued, and heard.

I think back to high school and remember those who sat by themselves at lunch time in the cafeteria; fellow students who were outcast or rejected from the "cool table". I wonder what, if any, facets of intersectionality applied. We can't possibly know for certain as there are invisible aspects to our identity too, but I imagine that one or several of these marginalized identities apply. If it doesn't feel good to reflect on these situations, you're not alone. It's hard because these memories conjure up feelings that in one way or another, we may have contributed to alienating others who were different in some way. Again, the intention of this perspective is not to shame or blame, but instead to expand perspectives and inspire different actions going forward. We can change today how we create and nurture environments of inclusivity and belonging for others. In *Humanizing Leadership*, we say **yes** to this responsibility and challenge knowing we will likely mis-step or mis-speak, **and** we will learn and keep going. As Ghandi so wisely said, *"be the change you want to see in the world."*

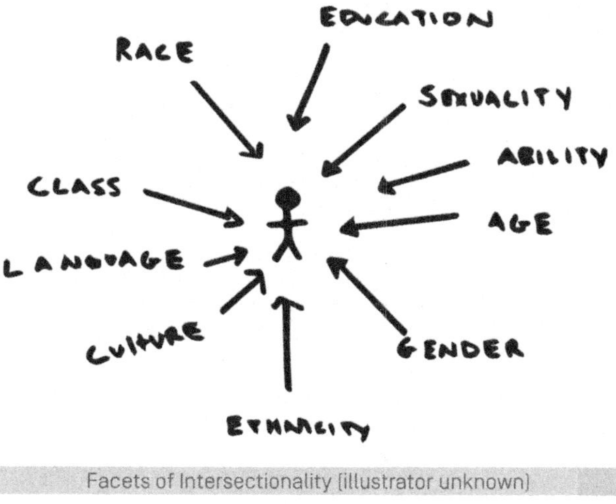

Facets of Intersectionality (illustrator unknown)

I interviewed an amazing human, Michelle O, on my *Humanizing Leadership* podcast where she shared the challenges of being a queer, middle-aged, anglophone black woman in a francophone city. The experiences she had in social and professional settings as a result of her intersectionality and intersecting identities have been very different from mine as a cis-gendered, middle-aged white woman living in a city where we speak my mother tongue. This is because in society, some identities are deemed more valuable than others. The greater the perceived value, the greater the power and privilege. This is a critical concept to explore and understand in order for us to make significant, meaningful progress on this journey of inclusion and belonging. And not just intellectually, but experientially. Otherwise the important DEIB work remains a box to check instead of meaningful change to realize.

Privilege

"Those who have the privilege to know have the duty to act."

Albert Einstein

Let's be clear. If life were a race of sorts, we are NOT all starting from the same start line. Some are starting much further behind, some much further ahead, from the moment we take our first breath out of the womb. Oxford Languages defines privilege as *a special right, advantage, or immunity granted, available only to a particular person or group.* What's hard, and I dare say impossible, to truly and fully understand, is the experience of those differently privileged. I've come to learn that many of the successes I've achieved in my life, and the failure of others, are not entirely fair; that while I have worked hard, some of my successes are in part because of where I started, and the apparent failure of others are in part because of where they started. It wasn't until 2013 that this door of awareness cracked open a little more for me where I ***felt*** what privilege was. It changed me forever.

I was a participant in a Diversity & Inclusion workshop where we were led through an exercise called The Privilege Walk [note: I don't recommend The Privilege Walk because it further marginalizes for the purpose of educating those not in a marginalized group.] The exercise started out with having all participants stand side by side in a straight line, all facing the same direction. The facilitator read a series of statements and after each statement would tell us how many steps forward or backward to take based on whether the statements were true/false for us. Some of the statements were:

- If English is your first language, take one step forward.
- If either of your parents graduated from college, take one step forward.
- If you have visible or invisible disabilities, take one step back.
- If you came from a supportive family environment, take one step forward.

As a white British-Canadian woman with well-educated parents from a middle class home, where do you think I was at the end of the exercise? Pretty darn close to the front. My range of emotions were broad, deep, varied, and conflicting. On the one hand I felt fortunate to be out in front – I had so many opportunities and experiences at my door. Life seemed great! But then I looked behind me, at all my friends who only through circumstance, were starting life way behind me. These were hard-working, smart people who grew up in a lower income bracket than I did, were BIPOC (Black, Indigenous, Persons of Colour), had a visible disability or another dimension that in our western society meant they were not afforded the same opportunities from the get go. This didn't feel right, just, fair, or good at all. In that moment I realized my being out in front, which represented my starting point in life, was pure circumstance. At this point in the exercise, after these questions were answered, I had yet to DO anything in my life to have gained this advantage. This was merely my starting point. And that was theirs too; not by fault or action of their own. Let me emphasize the point that I'm referring ONLY to one's starting point in life. This exercise focused on the circumstances we were born into. It did not then delve into what came next – the choice one exercised with what to do with the privileges one was afforded or the disadvantages one found themselves with.

The purpose was to ***experience*** the intricacies of privilege one is born into and to explore the ways that we enjoy privileges based on being members of certain identity groups in North America, if only in a classroom setting. To demonstrate how power and privilege have impacted our lives. To not simply hear about it or read about it, but feel it. It was in this workshop where I was first introduced to the concept of privilege and its role in this work. It underscored the complexity of creating inclusive workplaces and highlighted the importance of this work and the responsibility we all have (especially the privileged).

Since participating in this exercise, I've recognized that while I experienced great awareness, it further "othered" already marginalized groups. While "othering" was not a desired outcome of this work, it's ultimately what happened. You see, my learning relied on individuals within marginalized groups having to publicly express their stories. They didn't need to participate in this exercise to know what oppression looked like - they've been living it their whole lives. So learning for me and others with power, yes. But at what cost? More specifically, at ***whose*** expense? I'm not afraid of leaning into risk and discomfort, but only when it helps, not harms. And YIKES, this further harmed. Thankfully, this exercise isn't commonly used anymore. Instead there are exercises like "The Wheel of Privilege and Power" which provides a framework to reflect on our own privilege and power (or not) in an intersectional way. You do this in quiet reflection, as opposed to a group exercise that causes further harm to others already harmed. In this exercise there is an option share; an opportunity for marginalized individuals to take the space (and the mic) to share their lived experiences if they so choose. I wish to emphasize that I'm neck deep in this work myself and have so much more to do. But what I know for sure is that to humanize leadership, we need to advance this work.

It is not easy. Thankfully there are experts for whom this is their life's work. There are many educators and facilitators with lived experience who provide this service for individuals, teams and organizations. So find them, hire them, pay them. Put your google and social media skills to good use and find a professional to guide and educate you, your team and organization through this. There are so many people who over time have helped me in my journey. Some of these remarkable people include Michelle Osbourne[31], Saira Rao and Regina Jackson[32] and no doubt others along the way whose names mistake me. I humbly admit there are many dimensions of diversity I have yet to deeply educate myself on, but to omit this chapter from a book on Humanizing Leadership would be a mistake. This is foundational, not optional work.

Start your own personal journey and exploration TODAY. A great starting point is a tool (widely available on the internet) called "Dimensions of Diversity Wheel". Google it. Do the exercise. Discuss with a friend what you learned and what your takeaways are. Ask your leaders at work and your leader in HR what's being done in this space? What can you do from your sphere of influence to start meaningful conversation to initiate sustainable change?

This is hard and vulnerable work. And this is necessary if we're going to make a real difference in the lives of those we share space with, and certainly if we're wanting to create real change with our diversity and inclusion mandates, and not merely check the boxes, but make a better world for us and for future generations. Let's leave a legacy of love and connection, not hate and division.

---

[31] (n.d.). *Michelle Osbourne*. Michelle Osbourne. https://www.michelleosbourne.com/

[32] Jackson, R., & Rao, S. (2022). *White Women: Everything You Already Know About Your Own Racism and How to Do Better.* Penguin. https://www.amazon.ca/White-Women-Everything-Already-Racism/dp/0143136437

My appeal to you is that whatever your position of power and/or privilege, you help others prosper. Use your power and/or privilege for good. Bring people in and lift them up. Be open, expect difficult answers (even seek contradictory perspectives), truly listen for the purpose of understanding, thinking differently, do differently, help others shine. This is *Humanizing Leadership* in action.

Different Strokes for Different Folks

The workforce has changed a lot since the 1950s and while some of our policies have evolved, there's a lot more that can (and needs) to be done to remove the barriers that prevent all from having equal access and feeling true belonging. For instance, a male-dominated culture is more likely to emphasize the near-term costs of paid leave and overlook or downplay the longer term benefits. How different this conversation may be if there were more women at the table making the decisions. The fabric of our organizations is so much richer, deeper and diverse. Our workplaces, mindsets, systems, and structures all need to reflect this new reality before it is too late. We need to get busy growing or get busy dying. I know what I choose.

"New voices are necessary for continued innovation and with diverse perspectives come the added potential to appeal to a broader market.[33]" *What and who are these new voices; and how do they sound?* There are voices present but many have been silenced. This risk of speaking up has been far too great. People in history have been criticized (some even jailed or assassinated) for sharing their voice, and yet we will not progress in a meaningful way for humanity if we don't find the courage within to speak up. Humanized leaders know these voices need to be heard; to empower others to share, and encourage all to listen. They sound like the leader speaking up for their female employee who is

---

[33] (2018, October 8). What Everyone Needs to Know About Diversity in Tech. *Forbes*. https://www.forbes.com/sites/quora/2018/10/08/what-everyone-needs-to-know-about-diversity-in-tech/?sh=7783ba3a35ad

being held back from promotion because she is of child-bearing age; the father who is not interested in fast tracking his career because he has young kids and wants to leave every day from work at 5pm to spend time with them; the voice of someone with a learning disability who can share their perspective on why a new software feature may not work for customers of all abilities; the voice of a new immigrant who had to persevere and work hard to get to our country and has a valuable perspective to add to solving a problem from a different angle. "Companies with more culturally and ethnically diverse executive teams were 33% more likely to see better-than-average profits.[34]" (McKinsey Report, 2018).

I have ideas based on my research and experience about some of the strategies that need to be implemented, but I also know that no decision should be made by any one person; no single group should speak on behalf of or make decisions on behalf of another group. All voices need an equal seat at the table if they are expected to follow the rules; with the goal of creating a safe environment that welcomes all ideas, thoughts and points of view.

In the 1980s, there was a tampon commercial where young women were happily dancing around a meadow in white dresses. There was a suggestion of lightness and freedom for women who used this product while they were having their period. All the girls I knew at that time found that commercial laughable! We didn't know a single person who felt like that during 'that time of the month'. While I haven't validated this, it has been suggested that it was men who created the commercial. It sounds ridiculous now, yet this is what we do in so many of our boardrooms and businesses - make product and service choices and decisions for groups of individuals whose presence is missing from the decision making table.

---

[34] Dixon-Fyle, S., Hunt, D. V., Yee , L., & Prince , S. (2018, January 18). Delivering Through Diversity. *McKinsey.*

https://www.mckinsey.com/capabilities/people-and-organizational-performance/our-insights/delivering-through-diversity

When we're talking about initiatives and programs for new immigrants in our countries, those with disabilities, members of the LGBTQ+ communities, visible minorities - *who am I as a white, straight British-born-Canadian to be making decisions about what they need to be successful in our organization?* Instead of guessing what *they* need; ask. Involve. Empower. Invite all voices to be at the table, and not just the brainstorming table but the decision-making table too. When you look around that table and see a fair representation of those who are served, you'll know you're on the right track.

> *"You wouldn't make soup with just one thing in it and expect it to be good soup."*
>
> Tina Fey

The Bridge of Discomfort

It's ironic. As I was writing this section of the book I tried to find a more positive term to describe the bridge. I was searching for a word less prickly than "discomfort". In doing so I was trying to make you, the reader, more at ease while discussing the topic of discomfort. But let's call a spade a spade. Some topics and conversations are just plain uncomfortable. And that's ok! What matters more is what we do once we notice the discomfort. Do we turn away or turn toward? Quite naturally we turn away from it, our survival instinct at play. In the context of uncomfortable workplace situations and conversations, we don't want to rock the boat, say the wrong thing, offend or make someone feel bad. We also want to fit in. While we're wired to avoid (perceived or real) danger there is an overlay of cultural norms that influence our behaviors. There are some cultures for instance that are more direct communicators, others more indirect. Perhaps easiest to view it as a continuum. All this to say, what's uncomfortable for one is not necessarily uncomfortable for another. And as a result, I see a whole lot of stuff not being talked about, preventing us from bringing and being our best because it's uncomfortable. Instead safety and comfort is prioritized.

I seek to normalize discomfort, not just in relation to conversations of inclusion, but in leadership and workplaces more generally. When we connect with our heart, assume positive intent in others, and lean into courage, suddenly inviting others into uncomfortable conversations feels less threatening. Instead of being connected to information and technology, we connect to something much more powerful - each other.

Making friends with the feeling of discomfort will do us all a favour. We'll stop fighting and trying to fix discomfort. Instead, it will be more of an observation; a noticing ("oh - there it is again"), an acceptance of its presence. Then by applying the 1-2-3 Switch tool, we are able to mindfully, intentionally, and productively carry on. We now have a new way of relating to discomfort which gives rise to a new way of relating to one another. A new 'normal' that enables understanding, connection and growth.

When I was implementing a D&I strategy at a non-profit (it was only called diversity and inclusion at that time), I was asked to make sure that the dominant group was not too uncomfortable through the process. *Not too uncomfortable? When your beliefs, thinking and worldview gets challenged, how is that not uncomfortable?* I'm afraid to admit that I said "ok" to this request (and happy to report that I learned and grew from this experience). So how did I do? Did I make it comfortable? While I tried, it didn't work. Of course, they were uncomfortable! Those who reacted with fear because of the uncertainty this raised reacted like a scared cat in a corner - spitting, scratching, and hissing. *Did it work out in the end?* I'm not sure. I see the organization now and believe it's still on that journey. Upon reflection, had we approached it differently and expected equal discomfort alongside greater curiosity and connection, the journey could have been much more rewarding and successful.

What if instead we invite people to meet on the bridge of discomfort to have a conversation - a non-judgmental space between where they are and where we want them to be? Like "No Man's Land", a term used during wartime to describe land that is unoccupied. It's safe there on the bridge because it's there you can share, exchange ideas, reserve judgment and then decide which side of the bridge to walk to.

Compassion, courage, character and curiosity. Dropped assumptions, awareness of biases and a respect for the presence of blind spots. Together these create space for true inclusion - for being open to different perspectives, accepting others as they are, and actively seeking to include those within our society not represented on the bridge. It's about real people, real issues, real conversations, and co-created solutions.

Expect it. Express it. Elevate.

Our tolerance for discomfort needs some work my friends, and you as a leader play a key role. It starts with getting acquainted with the feelings of discomfort yourself, then encouraging others on your team to do the same. Demonstrate in your reaction that it's safe to do so. *Easier said than done?* You bet! When we feel uncomfortable we want that feeling to go away. We react quickly to get back to a better feeling state. Yet this is where I see the greatest opportunity for improvement in the area of inclusion. Discomfort brings up feelings of uncertainty and anxiety as our worldview and paradigm are shaken up before they reform into something new and better. In fact, it's in this discomfort that I found the bridge. We could meet on the bridge, putting down our own worldviews that we could pick back up if we want. There's no commitment required to cross the bridge; you're just willing to meet me on it. Here we connect with open minds, hearts, and curiosity. No judgment on the bridge. **Expect** discomfort and **express** it on the bridge. Inclusion starts with getting together.

When we assume positive intent and express our perspective on the bridge with compassion, respect and genuine curiosity for hearing the perspective of others, we create space for meaningful conversation. When we're working alongside others who are encouraged to assume positive intent, we can **elevate** our play as a team and in turn our results.

"We're quick to criticize (gender) injustice when we see it around the world. We also need to see it where most of us feel it and can do something about it - in the places we work."

Melinda Gates, The Moment of Lift

Cultivate a Culture of Authenticity

"For us to thrive professionally, especially in today's world, we must be willing to bring our whole selves to the work that we do. And, for the groups, teams, and organizations that we're a part of to truly succeed, it's essential to create an environment where people feel safe to bring all of who they are to work."

Mike Robbins, Bring Your Whole Self to Work.

Prior to the COVID-19 there was an invisible "coat check" as we entered our office each day where we hung up our home persona and put on our work persona. Similar to how Mr. Rogers on his children's daily TV show in the 70's, 80's and 90's would enter the set, switching from his outdoor shoes and coat to his indoor shoes and sweater. With the lines between work and home increasingly blurred, the "9 to 5" reality is long gone in many industries, certainly for knowledge workers. We're seeing the pressures of our personal and work lives increasingly spill over into one another in numerous ways; a merging of sorts with work creeping into the evenings after kids are in bed, chores done, or a good sweat at the gym has been had. We send emails in the wee hours of the morning before officially starting our day and before the family rises. We may even make regular mid-day personal appointments. It's the new reality and not going away anytime soon. If you consider when the 9 to 5 model of work was created, and who it was created for, you'll quickly realize it is an example of an outdated system that was created for employees at a certain time with specific needs. And it worked. The demographics of our workforce has since changed, as has technology and worker expectations. In fact, we have significant diversity in our workplaces today with respect to age, race, ethnic origin, religion, gender identity, sexual orientation, family status, abilities, etc. There is no one size fits all approach to meeting our diverse needs which means this antiquated approach to work getting done in the office between '9 and 5' needs to be retired. It's so ingrained in our mindsets and approaches that it's taken a global pandemic for this old paradigm to be shaken up, forcing us to rethink and redesign our entire approach to what work is, how and where it's done, and the role of the office. I recently heard a VP of HR at Ottawa based non-profit say: "work is what you do, not where you go." Yes!

The more we resist this new reality and continue wishing we could go back to the way things were, the more we suffer. The more we try to repeatedly force fit our expectations of what our life *should* be versus seeing life for what is and maximizing its potential, the more we continue to suffer. When we fail to accept change, the more stress and resistance we feel inside.

It's far more productive and less stressful to examine the resistance; then pivot. Organizations have come a long way but have so much further to go in how to approach, think about, and set up our systems, policies and processes to better support the changing reality. Many governments and established organizations that have existed for a long time without needing to modernize, have struggled more with this reality than new startups and tech companies who have had to adapt to survive. The COVID-19 pandemic has thrust many companies (along with their old paradigms and policies about how work gets done) into the future of work whether they were ready or not. Those that will thrive will be the ones who paused, reflected, and reimagined.

Work and life have merged and become so integrated with one another that I don't see how we go back. We can only grow forward. During the pandemic, I know we all got a glimpse into the lives of our colleagues in ways we never expected. I recall a time during a department-wide zoom meeting when the presenter paused briefly to knock on his living room window to stop his children from slamming a heavy metal shovel on their new stone walkway. There were barking dogs and noises from loud garbage trucks and construction vehicles. And yet our kids, our families, and "real life" have been here all along. Somehow being less visible they have been less considered by our leaders and organizations. During the pandemic there was no choice but to empathize and offer flexibility. Zoom rooms acted as an equalizer, humanizing our leaders and our workplaces. Our personal and family needs right there in front of us. And now as we emerge from the pandemic, we are living in a new work reality with employees bringing their values and redefined expectations to the table. As leaders we have an opportunity to check in and lead on:

- How can we as leaders take learnings from this situation? What are the learnings?
- What went well that you want to keep doing? What didn't that you want to discard? And what from the past is a thread you want to pull through to the "future of work" which is now?
- How can we continue to be exceedingly human when we find ourselves in a changed office environment?
- What good came from this unprecedented global experience?
- What glimpses did we see into the lives of our employees and colleagues that we need to remember and consider once we are away from home; back in our office spaces?
- How do we continue to support our people in a way that allows them to show up as their best self in ALL aspects of life, remembering what happens at work goes home and vice versa?
- What is within OUR control as leaders? What isn't?

Since the beginning of the pandemic I've heard many people romanticizing "When things get back to normal". There is no going back to normal. Do we ever really go back to anything? Do we want to? There are aspects I'd like to bring back, but I suggest we've learned too much and seen too much that there's no way we CAN go back. What if instead we considered growing into a new normal? What could we create that takes all the goodness of what we have learned and experienced about ourselves and others; about our need to be more compassionate, curious, and less judgmental; and about the need to take intentional effort at every level (individual, leadership, and organizational) to make our work environments both virtual and in person more human for all? Let's start with a big vision and architect from there. Yes there'll be barriers and realities that challenge us. But with an inspiring, co-created vision of the future, bright minds will figure out the how.

As I close out this chapter, there have been many personal reflections as I consider what's changed since I first started working in the D&I space. Perhaps what's most inspiring for me is that back then it was all talk about the business case. And yes, of course there are dollars and cents impacts that always need to be considered, but at that time the social justice piece carried little weight in the decision and conversation. Our society is finally and thankfully at a place where doing right by human beings is reason to do a thing. And the *Humanizing Leadership* approach to leadership enables it. I'm thankful that DEIB work now is about doing what's right for people, with people, and making it happen. That's the leadership our world needs today. It's also the kind of leader I aspire to be, people need, and we all deserve. So it doesn't matter about the latest method (although I'm always looking for a good book, a new technique or tool) - it's how you consistently, authentically, and vulnerably show up, step up and are seen. Every single day.

"Equality does not see colour, therefore, contributes to privilege. Equity sees colour, recognises systemic forms of racism and actively provided resources to level the playing field."

Sope Agbelusi

PILLAR 3: *Lead the Way*

Chapter 10.
Pursue Leadership Mastery

Welcome to the final section of the book and congratulations for getting here! This is the place where rubber hits the road; where all the pieces from Lead Self and Lead Others integrate and are embodied. It's about:

- becoming the leader you were meant to be,
- learning to be more of who you actually are, and
- leading with energy, optimism, and authenticity.

I want you to feel confident about bringing your whole self to leadership. While it's commonly said that leaders need to create cultures where their employees can bring their whole selves, this section shows how as a leader, YOU can do the same!

CHAPTER TEN

Pursue Leadership Mastery

As a leader, it goes without saying that you have a big vision. There are two ways to get people to follow. You can ***tell*** them what to do or ***inspire*** them to take action towards your vision. The authoritarian method uses force and fear to motivate people. What I'm sharing here is the co-creative method, where you inspire your team to share ownership of your vision.

Leadership mastery is something that evolves and surfaces as you develop awareness, apply skills, and relax into the essence of who you are. As an onlooker of someone who has mastered their trade (be it leadership or otherwise), it often looks easy and effortless. In reality, it's been years in the making. Likewise, as your essence merges with your self-awareness, competence and experience, a unique presence reveals itself. This is the expression of Humanizing Leadership. It takes intention, effort, time, and learning to develop into this, but to simplify, here's how you get there:

1. Know yourself by exploring who you truly are.
2. Master the art of no-bullshit relationships.
3. Be vulnerable and real by embracing your strengths and not fearing your failures or perceived weaknesses.
4. Spark curiosity by making your vision theirs.
5. Set the stage for others to lead and ignite the power of your team.

Leadership mastery is intangible but we know it when we see it. Rather than trying to explain this phenomenon any further, I thought I'd share a few examples of great leaders who personify it. As you read, make note of how they embody self-awareness, build authentic relationships, embrace vulnerability, spark curiosity, and empower others. My intention of sharing these examples isn't for you to take on the traits of other leaders, but instead to see how others have uniquely integrated these concepts with their own naturally emerging essence to lead with a unique and powerful presence. May it inspire you to lean into more of who you are and to bring that into your leadership each and every day.

Ruth Bader Ginsburg (RBG)

RGB was of strong moral character, grounded in who she was as a person and what she stood for, and was clear about what she expected of others. The boundaries of her relationships rooted in her own values were clear. She used this as one of her superpowers as fuel to create greater access and equity for women and men. She had a quiet confidence and was highly regarded and respected as an expert in her field. She had a big bold vision that extended beyond her own lifetime. Respectfully controversial, she pushed limits and boundaries all while maintaining positive relationships with others. She enlisted the hearts and minds of those in her profession, world leaders and the average citizen.

Through her vision, she has changed the face of gender equity in the world. She inspired generations of women to break down the barriers and obstacles in their own fields. She ultimately believed that everyone should be on equal footing and would stop at nothing to do that in her own profession. Let's consider how Ruth's essence was formed.

Ruth grew up in Brooklin in a lower-middle class family. Her mother Celia was forced to give up her own education to help pay for her brother's post-secondary education. Celia had different plans for her own daughter and taught her to be a lady and be independent, an unusual message for her time. Ruth's mother died of cancer the day before Ruth graduated from high school. Her early passing at the age of 48 was the catalyst for Ruth pursuing law as a career with focus and determination. This life-changing event led Ruth to live the life her mother could only dream about. "I pray that I may be all that she would have been," Ginsburg said, "had she lived in an age when women could aspire and achieve, and daughters are cherished as much as sons." This was her purpose and fuel; her bigger why and the well of courage that enabled her to continue her work despite ridicule and obstacles.

Her mother's vision became a vision for her life. She learned through loss what mattered and took up a cause that pushed her to be fiercely independent and know herself well to overcome the obstacles and inequalities of that time. She had to develop strength of character at a young age and know what she stood for.

Ruth started her work on equal rights in the 1950's, not a popular topic at that time. In fact it was termed her "Radical Project". She met much dissent, but still she persisted. So much so that she became known as a leading figure in gender discrimination litigation. Interestingly, many of her clients were men as her goal was to erase the distinction between men and women's rights/jobs. One key case was a man from New Jersey whose wife died in childbirth. The father wanted to work less and stay home with his son. He was met with a law that only allowed widows (not widowers) access to social security payments. RBG went to bat for him indicating this law was unconstitutional saying "laws of this nature keep women in a cage." She won. She wanted to shake up the preconceived notions of what it meant to raise families, contributing to the economy - she believed everyone should be on equal footing.

And shake she did. As a champion of liberal causes, especially equality for women, she designed and taught law courses on gender discrimination laws, was founding counsel for the American Civil Liberties Union's Women's Rights Project, and was a strong, outspoken voice with her Supreme Court colleagues. In 1993, at a count of 96-3, Ruth Bader Ginsburg was voted into the Supreme Court of the United States of America and served as associate justice until her death in 2020 at the age of 87.

She was only the second woman to serve on the Supreme Court. When asked when there'd be enough women on the Supreme Court bench (of which there are 9 seats) her response was "when there are nine."

RBG navigated vulnerability with grace and persisted in the face of tremendous odds. Her mere presence as a woman in law made her a target but she did not let that become a weakness. She believed change was possible and called on her strengths to nurture it, even though she was in the minority.

She was intellectual and incredibly hardworking, soft-spoken and subversively powerful. Through her work and unwavering protection of constitutional rights she fought her whole life for what she believed in - equality in law and in life. While she was passionate and relentless in advocating for her points of view, she also valued collegiality. RBG worked hard to find common ground with those she disagreed with. This is emotional intelligence in action. She felt the fury and frustration and channeled it as fuel to positively advocate for change. She had more than enough reason to be angry:

- Upon graduating from law school in 1959 (tied for top of her class) she struggled to find work because she was a woman and had a child. One of her law professors advocated for her and convinced a colleague to hire her for a clerkship.
- Following that, when she was offered a full time position at Rutgers School of Law (1963) she was offered a lower salary because her husband had a well paying job.

She didn't allow her hardships to harden her, but instead they propelled her to communicate in a way that inspired others to listen and act. She listened to others to understand their perspectives and differing viewpoints to which she would then respond with conviction and compelling, logical argument. She could only do this because she was being present, mindful, and aware. She was deliberate in choosing a way of connecting and communicating with others in order to bring about meaningful, positive change. What a beautiful example of meeting people on the bridge (inclusion). “When a thoughtless or unkind word is spoken, best tune out. Reacting in anger or annoyance will not advance one’s ability to persuade.” Ruth Bader Ginsberg

RBG was authentic and of strong moral character. She meant what she said, and did what she said. Her intention matched her words which matched her action. She stayed high when others went low, never meeting others with the rudeness or disrespect they may have shown her. RGB lived her beliefs and wasn’t afraid to voice them and yet she was artful in her delivery, careful to build bridges not chasms. “Fight for the things you care about but do it in a way that will lead others to join you.”

RBG’s way sparked curiosity and ultimately engaged people around the world to join her movement. In a time where many have finally woken to the need for equity across many different identity groups - groups that historically have been marginalized, oppressed, and overlooked - it’ll require us all to show up like RGB to make collective, positive change happen. May we all be as wise as RGB and do our part to “chip away” at legislation and practices that stand in the way of greater equity for all. Over the course of her career, she made huge strides against gender discrimination, but it was over many years and many Supreme Court cases. Leadership isn’t a one-time action - it’s a consistent way of being.

RBG blazed a trail through discrimination and set the stage for leaders to carry the torch for diversity, equity and inclusion. It has sparked advocacy in domains beyond gender and her legacy lives on through leaders of all ages around the world.

Jacinda Arden

Jacinda became New Zealand Prime Minister in 2017 at the age of 37, becoming the youngest PM in the country’s history in the last 150 years. Her style is one characterized by compassion, clear communication, and aligned action. It's how she builds trust and followership. She clearly demonstrated her value of unity, belonging, and decisiveness in the aftermath of a 2019 terror attack in her country where 51 Muslims were killed. "They are us," she said of the victims. Immediately following the attack, she implemented stricter gun laws. This bold move demonstrates her confidence and self-awareness which develops from knowing yourself.

Not long after, her leadership was tested yet again with the COVID-19 pandemic. And she did not disappoint. In fact she rose to the occasion and continued to show the world what is possible with a humanized approach to leadership. After the emergency alert was broadcast, she sympathized with the nation about how alarming the news was that life as they knew it was indefinitely over. She related to citizens citing real-life examples of how difficult it will be to avoid parks with our children because the virus could live on surfaces for many hours. She didn't pretend it was a short-term lockdown, but instead was honest about her expectation of it lasting for 10+ days and encouraged citizens not to be disheartened. Her no bull-shit communication did not sugar coat the situation but she inspired trust and confidence that the government was taking the right steps to keep the country safe.

She became known for her authentic facebook lives where citizens would get a peak into her life, seeing the life behind the leader. Dressed in sweats with a crying toddler and toys in the background, she embraced vulnerability and built further trust by showing that she was struggling just like everyone else.

Jacinda not only encourages others to be strong and be kind, she exemplifies it through her sincere communication. "Too much focus on power and strength means leaders can lose sight of the need for kindness." Her belief that empathy and strength can coexist in good leaders has sparked curiosity in people around the world.

She describes herself as relentlessly positive and so she was through the pandemic, leading her country with bold, decisive action while setting an example for other world leaders. She restricted travel earlier than most countries and very early on in the pandemic stated her goal of eradicating the virus - not merely controlling it. And so she did. Her style was to make it a community affair, calling citizens of the world her teammates. She was them. They were her. By setting the stage for others to lead regardless of their circumstance, she helped people all over discover their personal accountability, responsibility and control to impact their own reality. She created a genuine feeling and culture of belonging and togetherness even through crisis.

Dr. Martin Luther King Jr.

Such a well-known leader and difference maker, MLK was a baptist minister and American civil rights activist and leader from 1955 until his assassination in 1968. Born on the verge of the Great Depression to middle class parents with a strong sense of family, these years significantly defined who he became.

He was realistic and idealistic. "I think that my strong determination for justice comes from the very strong, dynamic personality of my father, and I would hope that the gentle aspect comes from a mother who is very gentle and sweet." His mother taught him that despite what others may say of him, he was worthy, he mattered, and he was as valuable as anyone else. He learned courage and confidence through this father. What he admired most in his dad was his integrity, and his moral and ethical principles.

Sitting at the dinner table at 6 years old, MLK came face to face with the reality of racism when he learned of a friend who was no longer allowed to play with him. This pivotal and poignant time in his life directed his future towards activism through words. At an early age he had to ask himself difficult questions, develop emotional intelligence and knowledge of himself.

MLK recalled another turning point in his life when he was shoe shopping with his father. They had been refused service because they would not sit at the back of the store. MLK's father told the store owner that they would buy the shoes sitting here or we will not buy the shoes. The fact that no aggression was exchanged showed MLK the distinction between the flawed system and the people within it. This developed his mastery of no bullshit communication.

Without question, sticking your neck out as a black man in the 1960s exposed you to immense hostility and danger. These were the ingredients necessary to effect real change in our world. MLK embraced this vulnerability with courage and conviction because in his mind there was no other way.

What could spark curiosity in an oppressed population more than the words of his paradigm shattering speech ..."I have a dream that one day this nation will rise up and live out the true meaning of its creed — we hold these truths to be self-evident: that all men are created equal."

His empowering words set the stage for leaders everywhere to summon their courage and stand by their convictions. To this day, as we embrace diversity, equity and inclusion, we still refer to MLK's provocative and inspiring words from so long ago. Today leaders in their own right and their own realms like Barack Obama and Stevie Wonder sought inspiration and courage from this incredible visionary.

Insert Your Name Here: ______________

What is your leadership story? What do you want it to be? Every day is a chance to start anew. All you need is the desire, an understanding of who you want to be, and a set of tools or guide to help you get there. With this book in hand, you are well on your way.

In closing, I'd like to leave with my mentor, Julia Wagg's, final words posted on social media for the world to see. May these words inspire you as they did me.

> "Do not wait until someone takes your time to make living your priority. I am so glad that I have known what it means to live with intention, presence, gratitude, and grace. It's the kind of insight that I wish I would have had inside of me years ago, and I hope you will leverage it to bring more depth and meaning to how you live now, too, and in whatever way that looks like for you."
>
> Julia Wagg

Julia Wagg, May 13, 1980 - April 14, 2017

Chapter 10 Sources

RBG

- (2020, September 19). *What We Can Learn From Ruth Bader Ginsburg*. Forbes. https://www.forbes.com/sites/rebekahbastian/2020/09/19/what-we-can-learn-from-ruth-bader-ginsburg/?sh=74391001fe8c

- (n.d.). *Ruth Bader Ginsburg*. Brittanica. https://www.britannica.com/biography/Ruth-Bader-Ginsburg

- 2020, September 20). *Justice Ginsburg Fought for Gender Equality. How Close Are We to Achieving That Goal?* New York Times. https://www.nytimes.com/2020/09/20/learning/ruth-bader-ginsburg-equality-vision.html

Jacinda Arden

- (2019, December 12). *New Zealand Volcano Eruption: Jacinda Arden Pays Tribute to Team Who Recovered Bodies*. The Guardian. https://www.theguardian.com/world/live/2019/dec/12/new-zealand-volcano-eruption-white-island-nz-police-victim-recovery-retrieval-operation-whakaari-live-news-latest-updates

Dr. Martin Luther King Jr.

- (2019, January 21). *Leadership Lessons from Dr. Martin Luther King Jr. Forbes*. https://www.forbes.com/sites/francesbridges/2019/01/21/5-leadership-lessons-from-dr-martin-luther-king-jr/?sh=1e3bc033279f

About the Author

With over two decades of experience in HR and talent management, Louise was driven to find a more effective approach to inspire individuals to excel in their work. Her extensive research, dedicated study, and persistent experimentation led her to a profound realization: the most exceptional teams emerge under leaders who actively encourage authenticity and wholehearted effort. Committed to fostering joyful, high-performance workplaces, Louise has dedicated her life to coaching leaders. When she's not coaching or facilitating workshops, you'll likely find her on the basketball court with her four sons or enjoying the great outdoors and quality time with friends on the golf course.

Printed in Great Britain
by Amazon

28382650R00116